LIBERTY IN THE
MODERN WORLD

The University of North Carolina Press
Chapel Hill, N. C.

The Baker and Taylor Co.
New York

Oxford University Press
London

Maruzen-Kabushiki-Kaisha
Tokyo

LIBERTY IN THE MODERN WORLD

BY

GEORGE BRYAN LOGAN, JR.

*"Die ganze Weltgeschichte nichts ist als
die Verwirklichung des Geistes und damit
die Entwickelung des Begriffs der Freiheit."*
—HEGEL

CHAPEL HILL

THE UNIVERSITY OF NORTH CAROLINA PRESS

1928

FOREWORD

There is a curious fallacy which should long ago have been exploded, not only by every war that has ever been, but also by the annals of all adventurous living—the notion that scholarly tastes and a love of letters on the one hand, and personal daring and the spirit of adventure on the other, are incompatible qualities. In George Logan, as in many another, they went hand in hand; and that is one reason why a brief sketch of his life should precede his book.

George Bryan Logan, Jr., was born in Allegheny, Pennsylvania, January 27, 1892, the son of George Bryan Logan and Frances Lyon Logan. He prepared for college in the Allegheny Preparatory School and entered Princeton in 1911, where he received his degree in 1915. He was recognized as one of the most brilliant men in his class and was graduated with final highest honors in English. He was managing editor of the *Nassau Literary Magazine* and a member of the Senior Council, and he had thoughts of a career as a writer—a hope for which poems of recognized promise had given distinct warrant. But by the end of his Senior year all plans but one, for him and for many of his like, had become of secondary moment.

And so in the month of his graduation, June, 1915, two years before his own country entered the war, he went to Serbia with a relief party organized by Professor Michael I. Pupin of Columbia University, under the auspices of the "Committee of Mercy." His work with this organization done, he was attached in September, 1915, to Lady Paget's hospital unit in Skoplje, Serbia, where his duties were those of orderly, dresser, and ambulance driver. In October, 1915, Skoplje fell into the hands of the Bulgarians, and Lady Paget

and her entire staff became prisoners of war until their release in March, 1916.

An extract from Logan's diary, kept for his family, gives a
graphic picture of the happenings at the occupation of Skoplje
and, quite unconsciously, reveals the insouciant spirit of adventure which was half his charm. Even torn from its con-
text, it tells more of him than many words of mine:

"The unearthly stillness had given place to a very real
crashing of big guns. From the hills to the north a giant was
hurling huge snowballs into Uskub, which flew splendidly to
pieces high in the air. I speeded home with very little loss of
time, at the foot of the Grad picking up three sisters who
appeared from behind a wall and flagged me wildly. In front
of the hospital I found marshalled two other cars. Tancock
and Osborn at the wheel, and Lady Paget standing beside
them. She explained hurriedly that our three cars were to
take the Bulgarian committee out to meet the advancing army
and ask the commander to stop shelling the city and the hospital at once. Somebody appeared with three American flags
and three bed-sheets, which were hammered to the sides of the
cars, and we drove off into town, Pavkovich going along to
explain our status. Two Serbian officers on horseback were
standing motionless at the crest of the hill to our left, using
their field-glasses. In 10 minutes we drew up abreast in the
deserted central square, and Pavkovich disappeared to round
up the various members of the committee. The air was full
of noise and white puffs of smoke, the Bulgars apparently
directing their fire chiefly against the railroad yards, the Grad,
and the road past the hospital, leading northwest to Pristina.
Pavkovich appeared, trailing behind him nine or ten individuals whom he affirmed to be the temporary dictators of
Macedonia. Their appearance was not prepossessing. Some
three of them, fat, clothed in frock coats and derby hats, and
festooned about the breast with long strings of medals, seemed
prepared at any moment to fly back into their cellars, and the
others, who reminded one of photographs of Pancho Villa
in his less prosperous days, looked as if they might have knives

in their boots. The leaders, including the chemist, a villain in a scrubby black beard, insisted on having chairs brought out and set in Osborn's car before they would ascend. Most of the latter crew piled in behind me and sat on the floor.

"So we set out, hardly knowing whether to fear most a bullet in the face or a surreptitious thrust in the back. We wound through the narrow streets of the Turkish quarter, catching half a glimpse at times of an evil face peering through a curtain, until we emerged into the country and the Kumanovo road, the ancient highway of the Crusaders. Two miles, running slowly, and we saw ahead of us a thin line of men stretching diagonally half a mile on either side of the road. Being uncertain whether they were Serbs or Bulgars, we slowed down still more, the committee jabbering excitedly to themselves in the rear. Suddenly three things happened: we discovered they wore brown and were advancing: we stopped: and the battle began with a tremendous flash of fire from their rifles. (We learned afterwards they had fired at us, thinking the automobile a ruse of the Serbs: but their sights were set for 1,500 yards and the bullets cleared out heads.) An interval of five inchoate seconds and then three complementary things happened: Osborn's car, which was in front, backed into mine and smashed the radiator; his three frockcoated committeemen tumbled, like Eli, backwards from their chairs, burned themselves on my hood, and lay flopping ridiculously in the mire; and the Serbs among the cemeteries answered with a terrific volley. Our position was not the most enviable. We were soon made to feel by both sides rather in the way, so we crawled severally through the mud to the side of the road and lay as unobtrusively as possible in the ditch, which I can swear was not more than four inches deep.

"During the next two hours three lines of the Bulgarian attack passed over us. The men, splendidly trained soldiers, would run up, fling themselves into the ditch beside us, fire half a dozen times, catch their breath, and trot forward toward the hill, while the officers blew their whistles, brandished their swords just as they do in colored lithographs, and yelled till their voices broke. It was war waged in the time-honored fashion, war as it should be waged, even in an unimportant rearguard action. Fifteen or 20 men would take refuge behind each of our cars, and it was against them that the Serbs seemed to concentrate their hottest fire. The rifle bullets whistled their droning scales about us; high above the big shells screamed by like a fast freight with all the brakes set, and the tearing shrapnel kept bursting on every side. Soon the Bulgars brought up a machine gun and began emptying it a hundred feet down the ditch. Then the Serbian shrapnel got a better range, and two pieces, falling on either side of me spattered me with mud at the same time. Did not like it, so squirmed down the ditch away from the cars, and saw little of the rest of the battle, observing chiefly the habits of the Macedonian ant and one corner of Tancock's boot, which latter gave me much comfort. Later a Bulgarian officer, who spoke German, sat on the edge of the ditch talking to us, and then charged forward with his men. A soldier, wounded in the arm and faint from loss of blood, lay down beside us, and we bandaged him as well as we could with handkerchiefs and adhesive we found in our pockets.

"When the third line was passing the firing seemed heavier than ever, but soon they drove the Serbs from the top of the hill and only an occasional bullet sang by. Tancock, Osborn and I dug ourselves out of the mud, with the help of a Red Cross soldier, who came up, lifted four wounded Bulgars into the two cars which, though somewhat mangled, were still serviceable, and we resumed our pilgrimage down the road. The committee had evaded. Along the ditch were lying a good many dead and wounded and alone in the midst of a field a crazed officer, his left leg red with blood, sat on horseback cursing and beating the animal violently about the head with his fists. Behind the first hill we came upon the reserve artillery, unlimbered, and the commanding officer with his staff, including two Austrian doctors, white-robed, rubber-gloved and bespectacled. Though we were too late to be of any service, we delivered our message in French; the commandant smiled politely, assured us the hospital and the city were in no danger whatsoever and offered us cognac. However, he kept us with him for half an hour before allowing us to go back.

"The retreat of the Serbs had begun, the firing had passed over the second hill, and the Bulgarian transport wagons were already going forward when we set out on our return journey. The road to town was crowded with Turks streaming out to welcome the 'army of liberation,' and our entrance became something in the nature of a triumphal procession. As we turned up by the stone bridge the first small body of troops to pass through the streets fell in behind us. Bulgarian flags had appeared magically at windows; the Turks, armed and swarming out of every house like prairie dogs, yelled and shot their guns into the air, the girls pelted the cars with flowers; the officer at the head of his men bowed graciously and in this comic opera manner we drove through free Uskub. Our cars were pushed madly up the long hill, but on the hospital road we were halted and surrounded by a mob of excited Turks who seemed equally ready to kiss our hands or knife us.

"They feared we were going off to join the Serbs on their retreat and would not let us continue for an hour or more, while we sat anxiously watching a huge pillar of smoke which rose above the hill where home should have been. Finally they cleared the road and we sped forward to see a score of haystacks, which the Serbs had fired as they went, blazing fiercely in a field behind the hospital buildings. We were received as from the grave by Lady Paget and the others; our wounded were hustled through the crowded bathroom and into bed, and we went in to dinner to hear the story of the Serbian retreat through the hospital grounds. Bulgarian patrols had been posted at the storerooms, and on the hill where five hours ago the two Serbian officers had sat we could see a little Austrian bolnichar marching proudly up and down with his newly-acquired rifle, keeping guard over his conquerors of yesterday.

"As I look out out of my window this evening I can see the city brilliantly lighted after its two nights in darkness. A good deal of firing is going on in the streets, mostly by way of jubilation, and a band is playing at Zirinski's. In the opposite direction the long line of haystacks is still smouldering, lighting up the field of battle fitfully. Beyond are the black mountains—and the Serbs. There will be hordes of wounded in tomorrow."

In April, 1916, after his release as prisoner of war, Logan returned to the United States, and from June to November, 1916, served in Texas with the Pennsylvania National Guard. But Texas was not the Front, and in January, 1917, he went to France as a volunteer with the American Ambulance Field Service. On account of his earlier experience he was transferred to the Macedonian Front, where, working with the French for the Serbs, he and his comrades in the Service drove nightly under constant shell fire to the dressing stations behind the lines. By this time the United States had entered the war, and in September, 1917, he returned to France and joined the American Air Service as a Flying Cadet. On May 16, 1918, he was commissioned First Lieutenant, American Air Service, Signal Reserve Corps. He saw service in France until March, 1919, when he was returned to the United States and honorably discharged, April 7, 1919.

During his training as an aviator he suffered a severe attack of cerebro-spinal meningitis, and though he recovered sufficiently to be retained in service, his health was permanently impaired. On his return to civil life, he entered his father's business in Pittsburgh, but his health gave way, and he was compelled to take up his residence temporarily in Florida. But it was not in him to remain idle, and in 1922 he entered the New York State Library School at Albany, and in the fall of 1923 became Librarian of the School of Education at the University of North Carolina, Chapel Hill, N. C. The following year he became Reference Librarian and Bibliographer at the same institution—a position which, together with the review editorship of the *Journal of Social Forces,* and the editorship of manuscripts for the Institute of Social Research, he held at the time of his death. He died of pneumonia on December 18, 1927. But his life had been given years before, in the service of his country.

He was married at Biarritz, France, August 13, 1918, to Agnes Mann, of Inverurie, Scotland, who, like himself, had early volunteered for relief service at the Front, and who, with four daughters, survives him.

The *Chapel Hill Weekly* of December 23, 1927, gives him as his later associates knew him:

"When George B. Logan died last week the University and Chapel Hill lost a man whose generosity and modesty and altogether lovable nature had won the hearts of all who knew him. He was self-effacing to the point of shyness, yet his exceptional charm permeated the whole community. He was the sort of man toward whom a stranger, after a few moments' conversation across the library desk, felt a warmth of affection such as is commonly accorded only to an old friend."

Something had been his of both his early loves—life at its keenest edge and the quiet companionship of books. And both had been characteristically transmuted into service.

JOHN LIVINGSTON LOWES

CONTENTS

LIBERTY IN THE
MODERN WORLD

CHAPTER I

THE MEANING OF LIBERTY

The better world has been one of man's most unquenchable and most elusive hopes. His attempts in all times to apprehend its foundations stand as a heritage for our own day that is at once splendid and sad. We can look back to almost every age and catch sight of those who have been oppressed by the cruelty, the waste, and the pride which seemed inseparable from society, and who have turned with all the strength at their command to oppose to these evils the ideal of a new basis and manner of living. The philosophers are among them, and the poets: we in the twentieth century are heirs alike of Plato and Augustine and More, of Isaiah and Shelley. But with them and after them stand we know not how many lesser men, who, lacking their high genius for expression, have yet experienced the same weariness, the same revulsion, and a vision of some like kind. Even the darkest generations of greed or cynicism have been unable wholly to break off the succession, though often enough the line has become faint and precarious.

This ideal of the better world and its counterpart for the individual, the good life, have been viewed from a number of different angles. In the two streams of ancient culture which we know most about, the means of realizing these ideals were comprehended broadly under conceptions that we may name justice and righteousness. Each of these conceptions was shaped by a fundamental attitude towards man's place in the universe and his possible destiny.

It was the Greeks who first saw human life as a mechanism of intricate design, acting ultimately under the fatal touch of forces not to be understood or controlled, yet capable of being brought, at certain times and places and by skillful arrangement of balances and authorities, to a delicate harmony, in which every man's desires and talents would hold a designated place. This view, the classic exposition of which is to be found in the *Republic* of Plato, looked to an unchanging, hierarchic society, living in and for the moment guided by a fixed principle (named justice by its first great exponent) which would bring about social security through a rigid system of duties and compensations.

The Hebrews moved in a very different universe. For them morality was to be found not within the world but without. To the greatest of their thinkers life appeared as a tremendous drama running through the centuries, its climax and catastrophe known from the beginning, a cosmic tragedy which could be relieved only by the surrender of human purposes to God and the cultivation of earthly interests under His immediate direction. The conception of society as a theocracy and of righteousness as man's knowledge of the divine will and obedience to it, were assumptions alike of law giver and prophet, however the people might differ in acting upon them. These two conceptions, which we may distinguish as the static and the dramatic, the mechanical and the personal, the aristocratic and the monarchic, have never ceased to color the thinking of the western world in later times, and both of them still remain as powerful though waning influences.

The distinctive ideal of our own day has found other expression. The modern man is apt to think of society as being in its nature neither static nor dramatic, but progressive; in its relationships neither mechanical nor personal, but organic; and in governance neither aristocratic nor monarchic, but democratic. Most of us have come to look at human life, however intricate and tremendous it may be, not as a piece of machinery to be tinkered with, nor as a vale of tears to be passed through as fearfully and prudently as possible, but as something worth cultivating and understanding for its own sake, as in some obscure way a living organism that must, for mastery, be continually bending and adjusting itself to its surroundings and its surroundings to itself. And in so working out its own salvation, it leans, not on any elaborate system of customs and institutions, nor on arbitrary authority of any sort, but on the collective experience and efforts of the individuals who have in all times made it up. As its goal we would be likely to set neither security nor obedience but the well-being and happiness of all its members; and as its means, a principle, a force, a process, which can be called by no other name than liberty.

Now these three roads to a finer way of life are not, or need not be, at war with one another. They are brave attempts to solve the same eternal problem, and the intelligent man of today, living in a world that has overtopped the Hellenic and Hebraic cultures while still drawing much of its strength from them, would say that liberty is large enough to take in the other two. It is, indeed, the Christian solution; for, though it has often worked through secular agencies for secular ends, it is yet the product of a temper in human affairs that was born and nurtured under the standard of the church. The great achievement of early Christendom was the fusion, in its own distinctive manner, of righteousness and justice, the coalescence of certain vital portions of Jewish religion and Greek thought which brought into being, under Roman and feudal government, a complicated but relatively stable medieval society. The great achievement of later Christendom has been the expression of ideas and the release of energies long implicit or latent in it, the emergence of free minds, free institutions, and free individuals that have broken up the medieval world into a society not stable, but vigorously alive and possessed of a new and potent principle of living.

It is, we dare to say, a wider principle than others which came before it. For behind the organic world so astonishingly revealed to us in modern times, we are beginning to discern certain groups of laws that we would do well to understand and obey, if this continuous, corporate life of ours is to go on successfully. They are the laws of our physical environment, the laws of human association, and the laws of our inner nature. Now the idea of justice has concerned itself, in what seems to us a curiously stiff and narrow way, only with the second of these groups of laws. The idea of righteousness has fixed on certain of the third of them and subjected the first and second to these in a manner that has never failed to distort and restrict human activities. Both ideas are valid within their true limits; and they are the steps by which the mind of man has come to its present estate. But liberty, as it may be defined here, consists in the fullest and freest adaptation of man's character, faculties, and habits to the world of nature, the world of his fellows, and the central world of consciousness, and his resulting use of them all, in so far as he is able to use them, for his own good. It is justice and righteousness; but it becomes, as well, material power and social community and the worth of the individual and the fruits of the spirit. It is, in the broadest sense, accepting the universe, putting the most into it and getting the most out of it, all the while feeling ourselves normal and inevitable parts of the whole. Under such an aegis we may some day come to feel altogether at home on this earthly sphere.

In one basic assumption the idea of liberty differs from the views of other times. It takes for granted the possibility of progress—or as we may prefer to call it, the evolutionary scheme. Whatever we may think of evolution as a biologic fact or a universal tendency, most of us have come to assume that human affairs may be so comprehended and so ordered as to move perceptibly, within what limits we do not know, toward the greater happiness of the individual and the race. We are not always aware of the daring and revolutionary character of this new concept. It used to be supposed that all life stood still or was destined to degeneration or at most swung in hopeless recurrent cycles. In defense of these cosmologies, voices worth listening to are still raised; but to them the better world can be hardly more than a precarious conservation of past values or the scene of fitting preparation for a life to come. For several hundred years men have felt dimly that society was a growing thing, capable of further conscious development, and that it was within human power to find the terms under which such development might take place. The startling discoveries of biologists in the last century have given new scope and meaning to these earlier speculations and have helped to broaden them into something like a popular faith. Evolution does not, of course, imply progress; but when man has decided what road he wants to travel and is prepared to use the forces of change to impel him in the right direction, the two may become all but identical. Progress is, after all, only a guess: we cannot see clearly enough into the past or control the present completely enough to know whether man has ever advanced, or is now capable of advancing, in happiness and the well-being of his whole nature. But it is a brilliant and fascinating guess, well worth testing for a few generations, that by the use of freedom we might make ourselves masters of our destiny. It is hardly true, as has been finely, if rather exaggeratedly said, that man is today "the spectator of all time and of all existence"; but he has caught the idea of human history as a flowing stream that can perhaps be guided nearer to his heart's desire, and there have come to his hand some of the means for so guiding it. This new inspiration belongs to him as an individual and as a member of all his varied communities; it is a double adventure in personal and social responsibility. He is at last beginning to take for his watchwords, self-knowledge and self-control.

Like most other things, our utopias have suffered a change. The ideal societies of earlier days were exercises of the imagination unhampered by fact, heroic flights into the impossible. It is not likely that any of their authors thought them realizable. But when the aspiration of yesterday becomes the actuality of today, as we see it becoming all about us, a partial and limited utopia is constructed before our eyes; and if a partial and limited utopia, why not, line upon line, as we gain in knowledge and power, a complete and all-inclusive one? We are no longer willing to segregate our philosopher-kings and creative citizens in the sun or on a remote island; we are hoping, on the contrary, to learn through them the reasonable and possible principles of a harmoniously developing social order which knows its own mind and is not satisfied with the objectives it has already reached. And if we are to be the architects of our own future, we need all the freedom we can get to build it.

Liberty, we have said, is not an end but a means. It is not a program of human betterment, but a process under which men, individually and in society, may develop most fully their own capabilities. It is a force which calls out and directs our energies for the attainment of certain results. Liberty in a vacuum is without meaning: only as the power inherent in it is applied to definite problems and fields of human interest can it evoke the loyalties of men and play a part in history. For freedom as a metaphysical term, few care except the metaphysicians; but for the freedom of particular actions and institutions and ideas, men by the thousands have been willing to lay down their lives.

Certain other things, we need scarcely be reminded, liberty is not. It is not equality; and although in certain areas of social life it can best be maintained by the equal use of specific powers and functions, the two have no necessary connection. Equality wears as many different faces as liberty itself, and its meanings need to be as rigorously defined; but in the larger sense of the uniformity of all human activities and relations it is abhorrent to a principle that rests on the flexibility and diverse richness of life. Liberty must in fact often become the bulwark and guarantor of inequality, of the opportunity of every man to cultivate his own peculiar talents and find his natural level in society. Nor does liberty mean merely doing as one pleases. On the contrary, it acts toward a sensitive, if fluid, adjustment of conflicting rights and interests, under which certain desirable things must be given up in order that others more desirable may be secured, and freedom of every sort, perhaps, denied to some men, in order that greater numbers may enjoy it more fully. Hence, liberty can persist only under discipline that is the more authoritative because it is self-imposed. Nor, again, is it a breaking with all familiar customs and habits in order to launch out over uncharted seas. Liberty has its history, its traditions, its methods, and its materials, inherited from other days, all woven into the texture of our present lives; and it looks backwards as often as forwards for help in time of need. "There has hardly been any great forward movement of humanity," wrote Gilbert Murray, "which did not draw inspiration from the knowledge or the idealization of the past."

Lord Acton, one of the profoundest scholars of the last century, spent most of his life in accumulating a great mass of literature, from every age and country, bearing on the development of thought, the struggles of creeds and institutions, the growth and subsidence of ideals. All this was to be the material for a history of liberty, "the emancipation of Conscience from Power, and the gradual substitution of Freedom for Force in the government of men." After forty years of preparation, he died before the results of his labor could be given to the world, and no later historian has ventured to take up and carry to completion the unfinished task.

One wonders whether the task will ever be done. In this time of restless disillusion, such a work would help us to look at the world we live in with renewed steadiness and singleness of vision. Liberty is, in a way, a touchstone for the integrity of life: its history means little less than the history of enlightenment. Of the forces working in and shaping the modern world, this is one of the strongest; man's attempt to capture and harness it in his own service comprehends a good part of his mind and the extent of his will into the future. The freedom of the individual, the freedom of the corporate mass, and the swaying balance of the one against the other are prime realities in the unfolding of social consciousness and social control.

The spirit of liberty is one of the true master currents driving ahead through modern life, sometimes beneath the surface, but never completely lost or turned aside; its dynamics belong among the deeper impulses of human character. In it have been concentrated the cardinal issues of society since the close of the Middle Ages. It could be made to yield as simple and as large a view of our civilization as we are likely to get—the only view, it may be, that could piece together a disjointed and uneasy prospect. Nothing else would so light up what Victor Hugo called the venerable duel of the fact and the right, the age-long conflict between the world that might be and the world that so discouragingly and persistently is.

Through what agencies does the principle of freedom function toward the improvement of human life? Two possibilities may be disregarded with a fairly clear conscience. The possibility that man's physical or intellectual faculties can be so radically altered and developed as to reach out into hitherto unguessed fields of activity is decidedly remote. The possibility of a more general approach to the fullest powers yet known, through further sharpening of education and selection, there may perhaps be, but conceivably no new range of capability, no hidden springs of energy are yet to be tapped. Our models must still be the Greek athlete and the Greek thinker—and would perhaps be the Cro-Magnon hunter and artist if we knew them better. No more than a barely appreciable change in the bodily or mental constitution of men has been observed in the last two or three milleniums, and such change as there has been is nothing to boast of. If anything larger is possible, we are unable, save in the tragic farce of the superman, to imagine what it may be, or whither it would lead, in spite of the evolutionary color of our present thinking. Man's body and mind in themselves are scarcely to be considered the vehicles of a better way of life.

Eliminating then, these visionary fancies, four practical possibilities present themselves. There is the recasting of the larger institutions under which man lives, the more rational ordering of society with respect to the intricate relationships of status and contract that may exist between different communities and individuals. There is the conquest of the forces and materials of nature, with the eventual subjection to our will of the immense resources which invention and discovery are continually and with increasing prodigality laying bare. There is the reverent understanding of man as the possessor of a unique personality which is, in a very real sense, the measure of all things, and such readjustment of the more intimate affairs of his life as will distinguish and dignify all he is and does. And lastly, by the recognition of man as a being whose most real and important existence goes on beyond reach of the senses and the intellect, there will be so complete an assertion of his spiritual nature that it at once becomes the final arbiter of his outward life and the home of a more abundant life within. These forces of change have been submitted to endless variety of application in different times and among diverse modes of thought. Through their translation into programs of action they may explain a good deal—*Das Kapital,* for instance, and the farmers at Concord Bridge, Lewisite and chaulmoogra oil, free love and the Positivist calendar, the Spanish Inquisition and George Fox's leathern suit. In the broadest terms they may be called social reform, natural science, humanism, and religion.

There is material here for many volumes in the grand manner. Only the fringes of the subject can be skirted in this essay. The five following chapters attempt to trace, in bare outline, the main currents of social and institutional reorganization in western life since the Middle Ages, while the last three chapters try to suggest some of the implications of scientific achievement, of the humanistic spirit, and of modern religion. Each of these—science, humanism, and religion—has fallen in some degree under the shadow of the recklessness, the hypocrisy, and the greed that are everywhere lying in wait to appropriate the fruits of human effort; but each has fallen also, and to a very large extent, under the more generous and invigorating influences making for progress and happiness. In so far as they have been allied with the liberating forces of the modern world, they take on the four aspects of social freedom, material freedom, moral freedom, and spiritual freedom.

By far the most widely accepted of these agencies of progress has been the first—the idea that by recasting the visible forms linking men together in society and thus altering their accepted rights and duties and loyalties, a finer and happier way of life can be built up. There are a number of reasons why this has proved so attractive. It is simple and clear enough to commend itself to the intelligence of the common man. It has dealt largely with institutions and with the broader principles that uphold them, on the assumption that what has been humanly constructed can be rebuilt or replaced to advantage by the wisdom of another generation. It is capable of such flexibility and such repeated modification in practice, that it encourages the method of trial and error and seems to promise satisfaction, at some time, to all those whose social theories or practical interests are concerned with it. It sways great numbers of restless, unsuccessful, or embittered men, who accept the chance to gain much and lose little under such new conditions as it brings about. It appears to have been used with striking success in the past and to be responsible for some of the most notable improvements over older ways of life. But most of all it appeals to the desire of every man for personal freedom, for overcoming those limitations and repressions which seem at every turn to prevent him from realizing the sort of life he would like to live. This is the secret of its strength. Throughout its history this idea has been a servant of liberty, one of the special energies generated under the action of that potent influence. Restricted to political activity, it had a long and adventurous career in ancient times, but a dozen centuries of conformity so cut off its past that the threads had to be taken up anew in the modern age. We are to see here how it has escaped from the world of imagination into the world of events, how it has been translated into a force that can overturn the principalities and powers of our daily life.

CHAPTER II

LIBERTY AND LAW

Social liberty is of course no abstract right but a principle based on its usefulness, in the long run and in the highest sense, to all men. A process whereby order can be combined with progress, its conditions have to be redetermined and reasserted by every changing generation. Acquiesced in, even for a little while, it becomes too rigid to meet the needs of a new time, and its virtue is quickly lost.

Never in the modern world has liberty been lost beyond recovery. The continual redetermination and reassertion of the terms under which it can live—that is, the making of our own free institutions—constitute perhaps the most heroic of human epics. We know, for example, that the fourteenth century was a time of radical realignment in civil life, the sixteenth century a time of religious upheaval, the late eighteenth and early nineteenth centuries periods of political conflict, the present day a time of industrial strife. These periods of crisis mark the culmination of long, slowly gathering movements that broke suddenly into the forefront of the world's interest. Each period marks a stage in the unfolding of a society in all outward respects its own master. Through cycles to be measured not in years, but in hundreds of years, our ancestors have fought out in succession the great battles whose results have secured (dare we say?) freedom of law, freedom of thought and expression, freedom of government; and we are now seemingly entered upon a fourth momentous struggle for freedom of work, the outcome of which lies beyond our sight. The goal has not been liberty for its own sake, but liberty employed in the advancement of certain particular causes—causes so powerful that many of the most ancient habits and institutions of their times have gone down before them. Hence the story of freedom must often be one of destruction, a series of conflagrations, in the midst of which, however, a new creature may be seen, phoenix-like, rising half-blindly from the ashes of a crumbling order. These revolutions are a part of our inheritance; we are living in the midst of one; and the rekindled fires of those whose first heat has passed, we are still sometimes called upon to face.

For a good many hundreds of years Europe's chief business was to fight for its very existence. From the gradual dissolution of the Roman world-state until well into the eleventh century there went on an almost continuous battle between the half-barbarous peoples who had first taken the territory of the decaying empire and the more sinister forces that pressed in on them from without. Above their own internal warfare, bitter though it often was, rose this struggle to preserve the elements of their culture and religion and to ward off the ever-present fear of annihilation that was the greatest bar to any real advance in civilization. The peaks of the long conflict we call turning-points in history: Aetius against the Huns—the last great effort of the old order and the first effort of the new; three hundred years later, Charles Martel and his Franks against the Saracens; and the sustained perils of the two centuries after Charlemagne, when western Europe beat back almost at the same time the crowds of Norse, Hungarian, and Arab invaders that swept down from the north, the east, and the south. As late as the thirteenth century the irruption of the Mongol hordes into the center of the continent threatened with extinction all that the Middle Ages had been able to construct and consolidate out of the preceding darker time.

The recoil of the Tartar horsemen from the forests of Ger-

many ended that critical period of European history in which
its newer peoples had won and re-won for themselves a precarious freedom of life. During the centuries preceding this
last threat of alien subjection, medieval society had been developing its own distinctive culture; and the Crusades, in
which the West became for the first time the attacker, dramatically marked the turn of the tide. But even the modern
world has not been able to shake off for good and all the menace of destruction. Twice in later times the old fear has raised
its head: when the victorious Turks lay before the walls of
Vienna, and in the twentieth century, when Europe appeared in danger of becoming her own destroyer. The nations
that fought the Great War, waged with new weapons, but
in so many quarters with the old aims, may have been equally
trained in the ways of civilization; yet, in so far as they used
their skill toward more ingenious destruction and prostituted
it to the ruthless triumph of arms, they showed themselves
true heirs of those earlier invaders who, time and again, had
all but captured the destiny of the continent. And the cataclysm we witnessed in Russia released forces and aroused
passions which may utterly disrupt from within the ordered
world we have known. Toward the end of the eighteenth
century, Gibbon, out of a sweeping knowledge of the past,
congratulated his age that the barbarians were extinct. We
are less sure, having seen barbarism in our midst—in ourselves, perhaps. Social revolution and modern war revealed
it to us. And we find new terrors in our uncertainty of the
uses which the quick and prolific colored races will make of
our scientific engines and our own example. The danger of ex-
termination by the aggression of armed, plunder-seeking hosts
is still with us. One of the most desperate of all present
problems is the preservation of this elementary freedom of
common life.

It was preserved in the first place and for a long time by those two agencies of social control we know as feudalism and the Roman Church. Feudalism was the later of these to be developed and the first to break down. At once a land policy, a social system, a code of morals, and a military organization, it rose in a rough age as the only means of defending Europe in face of the forces that threatened her. A type of organized life intervening between the old tribal systems, suited only to a primitive society, and the national states of later times, it became during this transition the preserver of relative order and security. By strictly formulating the group principles of man's relation to his fellows, it made the corporation its social unit; and the individual could exist only as he filled a recognized place in some corporation—manor, borough, guild, monastery, or chivalric order. Demoralization was met by a sweeping denial of personal liberty in a day when personal liberty would almost certainly have thrown the western world back into complete anarchy. The old empire was a fading memory, impossible to reconstruct on any broad or enduring lines; feudalism gained its ends, good or ill, by a thorough decentralization of authority. Government was regarded not as a public affair, still less as a public trust, but as the private property of kings, delegated largely to great nobles and by them sub-let to lesser feudatories, with military or personal services by way of payment. Law became a local institution, varying with each large district and sometimes with each fief. There was no equality of the law or before the law: the church, the merchant guilds, and the remnants of ancient popular administrative units maintained courts, each with its own rules and practices, in addition to the baronial and royal courts, and a man's rights depended upon his position in society or the unrecorded custom of the neighborhood. There was thus constructed a system of fixed status under elaborate gradations, in which the empty name of Roman citizenship and the free aristocracy of the barbarian peoples were alike merged and lost.

Feudalism belonged to an age of warfare. It could not long survive the disappearance of the conditions which had created it. When the frenzy of the crusades and the threats of pagan domination were over, men began to chafe under the restrictions it laid upon their new activities; and as their mental horizons widened, they saw on what irresponsible and abusive powers it often rested. In the brilliant and thoughtful life of the thirteenth century came the first signs that the usefulness of feudalism was passing. That age witnessed what was, on the whole, the most complete organization and highest development of medieval life. Its leaders—ambitious monarchs, subtle theologians, saints, artists and builders of genius—were conservatives who attempted for the last time the maintenance of society on a paternalistic basis. But beneath the surface, forces were working which were to take society out of their control. Already a link was in process of being forged, one that would join individuals and communities in a more just and congenial relationship than had been possible before. The most powerful and far-reaching of these forces was the new conception of civil law.

The great code of Justinian, which summed up the principles and methods of Roman jurisprudence just at the moment when it became impossible to apply them in the barbarian West, remained almost unknown there for more than five hundred years. Its study was revived, toward the close of the eleventh century, in the turbulent cities of north Italy. Thence it spread through France and Spain and Scotland, gradually modifying or replacing the old tribal and feudal customs, and in the process being itself widely modified by them. After a long battle with medievalism in Germany, it at last won there its most unqualified acceptance. In England, though the method and spirit of Roman law had great influence, its actual contents were swamped by the new body of constitutions and writs and decisions which during these centuries were so vigorously formulating the common law of the realm. But everywhere, through a period reaching in various countries over five centuries, the broader results were the same: the lineaments of our modern legal systems began to appear. The idea became general among the new class of lawyers—the first learned laymen—that law is neither a fixed compilation of ancient custom nor the arbitrary command of a sovereign, but that it exists as a body of practical logic, applicable to men's relations toward one another and toward their communities, and capable of growth and adjustment to varying needs. Against such a position feudal authority could not long stand.

England solved most notably the great problems of law: to discover law, to declare it definitely, and to enforce it without favor; and it is therefore in England that civil liberty first rose and has been most secure. Magna Charta put the king clearly under the law—then a conservative feudal law, but already in process of becoming something very different. For, during the thirteenth and fourteenth centuries baronial, commercial, and in less degree church courts were giving way before a single hierarchy resting its authority directly in the crown, until the royal jurisdiction came to replace all the diversified and overlapping jurisdictions of earlier times. Statutes were issued which began to alter the immemorial substance of law. Distinction was made between private and public law. Civil and criminal proceedings were separated. Ownership, rent, and alienation of land superseded the complicated feudal tenures. Personal property was more elaborately safeguarded, and laws of contract and tort began to be formulated. Trial by jury took the place of the old clearance by oath and the barbarous expedients of combat and ordeal. Out of all these changes emerged the principle of civil freedom—a law common to the nation, which bore equally on all men, under which all men possessed the same freedom of action and right to property, and by which the subject was protected from the arbitrary interference of government. A society that had lived largely by status began to live, in important respects, under contract, and a shadow of the old Teutonic personal liberty reappeared. "One people under one law" became a boast that had more than a little basis in fact.

But it could not be made without the memory of blood and bitter repression. No general or specific rights were handed down graciously to the common people: they had to be fought for. Nobles and merchants and burghers might bully or buy them from a needy monarch in special charters, but for the serfs on the soil, who had scarcely any legal existence at all, there seemed no recourse but violence. The expansion of the law to take in the great masses of every land, in whatever century it has come, is one of the two great movements that merged the Middle Ages into modern times. It was preceded by fierce peasant risings in France, England, Germany, Poland, and Switzerland. The process may be traced, first and most strikingly, in the England of the thirteen and fourteen hundreds, through the great pestilence that swept the country, the agricultural chaos that followed it, the panic of the landlords and the series of repressive enactments from Parliament, the revolt of the countrymen, its failure, and the quiet gain, in the succeeding decades, of all that had apparently been lost.

Here, for perhaps the first time, are the ominous portents of a modern revolution. We regard John Ball and Wat Tyler as provokers of the crisis: they focused the inarticulate questionings of many years to definite purpose and direction and once and for all flung the submerged hopes of their class into action. The beginnings were many years in the past and the materials ready to their hands. Before the serfs of England confronted the king at Mile End and Smithfield, their social moorings had long been torn up by the Black Death; loss of population had doubled the market value of labor, respect for the authority of the landholding barons was weakened, the incentive to steady work had disappeared—the country was rapidly drifting toward a state which could be resolved only by drastic reform or civil war. The time had its critic and prophet in Langland, brooding sullenly over corruption in high places and meanness in low, a somber realist who exposed in vivid cross section the unstable society he knew.

The first aim of the rebels was the abolition of serfdom, with commutation of existing feudal dues for an annual rent on land. Their demands were conceded, and charters to that effect were drawn up and sealed by the king. But the more determined leaders of the peasants, disregarding the new privileges, embarked on a brief career of murder and arson and later presented their far more extreme program calling for the removal of all differences of rank, status, and property in the kingdom. The young king, Richard II, appears to have been throughout a mediating influence, offering to put himself at the head of the insurgents to secure them their rights. But with the burghers turned against them and the London militia in arms, the rebels collapsed: the peasants were dispersed, their leaders hanged, and the next parliament voted truculently that all the charters granted by the king were void. The rebellion, falling, as so many rebellions have fallen, into more radical and more ruthless hands, could not secure even its earlier moderate aims, and many landlords used the ensuing reaction to revindicate their ancient claims.

But the spirit of the day was against them. The disappearance of serfdom was brought about, like all the major revolutions, by an involuntary alliance of forces in many fields—economic, political, social, and religious—with the widening consciousness of men. Throughout the fifteenth century the lords of the manor were losing many of their useful functions. Power was passing from the landed to the commercial interests of the nation; cities, jealous of their rights, arose with the new manufactures which attracted the labor of the countryside by a money wage; the king grew in strength at the expense of his nobles, by means of direct taxation, paid armies, and the royal courts, which, in their interpretations of the law, hastened the dissolution of an outworn manorial society. Under these conditions feudal administration and the feudal idea faltered. On the land, vague and indefinite personal services were transformed into clearly expressed and limited ones, and these into payments of money, until the normal type of peasantry came to be the prosperous renting farmers for so long the backbone of the realm. The sense of law, as a substitute for unchecked will or mere tradition, began to be a part of the mental habit of men. Villeinage as a personal status was all but destroyed, and its victims became freemen who learned to be proudly jealous of their one great equality with the most powerful baron.

Yet this victory of law over arbitrary or customary power is a long process which has nowhere been completed. Its beginning we have seen in England; the other nations of western Europe followed at varying intervals and by methods of their own. Feudal privilege, with its civil disabilities for certain groups of men, has held on grimly. There were still a few villeins bound to the English soil in Milton's day and to the Scottish coal mines in Burns's. A more or less formal serfdom survived in parts of France and Savoy until the

Revolution. In Germany it was not abolished until the nineteenth century and in Austria, Hungary, and Russia not until the second half of the century. As peonage it still persists over wide regions of Latin America and sporadically or under cover elsewhere. In our own Southern states a recrudescence of slave power on the Roman model for more than two hundred years refused the most elementary human rights to millions of a defenseless people brought into the country for agricultural exploitation.

Moreover, as distinct from political rights, civil liberty was for a long time, and sometimes still is, limited in respect of other classes, for some of whom the problem of securing it has been complicated by prejudices of a different sort. Catholics in Protestant countries and Protestants in Catholic countries have been denied it on account of religion; the yellow and brown peoples because of race; the Jews for either or both of these reasons. Until the early nineteenth century, no Englishman unable to read could plead before the law the privileged position of benefit of clergy. Indentured servants, who bound themselves to temporary serfdom for a passage to the New World, were familiar figures in American life up to the Revolution. A little more than a hundred years ago, brutal press gangs were combing the streets of English cities to dragoon luckless youths into the navy or merchant marine—the sea, indeed, remains today one of the last strongholds of tyranny. It has not been long since capital punishment, torture, and transportation for petty crimes were abolished, and the "third degree," together with other lawlessness of our police officers, is with us yet. Poverty, unpopular opinions, and even the keeping of bad company may only too often mean denial of justice in the courts to those who need it most. Woman has everywhere, in the most enlightened countries, come into the twentieth century with the shreds and tatters of her ancient degradation still hanging about her. And in modern war many civil rights are, by all but universal consent, and seemingly of bitter necessity, sacrificed to national safety, having afterwards to be revindicated at no little cost. The battle begun in the Middle Ages is still far from won.

We have been speaking so far of civil liberty as wholly a personal possession, and so it remained until well into the nineteenth century. But just as the commercial revolution demanded, and was accompanied by, the legal freedom of the individual, which replaced the fixed corporate life of the Middle Ages, so in our own day the industrial revolution has made necessary a new communal freedom under the law as a protection from unchecked individualism. During the last three or four generations public interest no less than private right has begun to be recognized as a proper ground for legal restriction on individual acts. And it is clear that the public interest may often be sustained only at the expense of certain aspects of the older personal freedom. The British factory acts of 1802 were the first recognition of this necessity for limiting certain rights of the few for the good of a much larger number; and since their day, laws relating to public health, safety, working conditions, industrial contracts, the care of women and children, and a host of other relationships have been based on the same principle. As other countries have entered upon the complexity of an industrial age, in which the power of a single careless or ruthless man to injure his neighbors, his city, or his nation becomes amazingly magnified, the same progressive revision of liberty has occurred. And although its every extension is opposed by champions of the older tradition, but few will still question the need for some measure of protection for the community as a whole and for its weaker citizens. So quietly, so inevitably has this revolution in our thinking come, that it is difficult to realize the extent to which, as one of the greatest English Tories remarked, we have all become Socialists. The struggle therefore revolves today about the proper balance between the civil rights of the individual acting solely in his own interest and the rights of many individual members of society considered as a group—a balance that will, on the one hand, avoid the perils of complete laissez faire and, on the other, eliminate the dangers of legal despotism. That we may never succeed in striking the happy mean is no reason to doubt the value of both elements in a splendid heritage.

A splendid heritage it is, for in rightful character, law stands as the most venerable and one of the surest guarantees of social stability. If it cannot directly bring about progress, it is the foundation on which all progress builds. It may, as the organized agency for expressing the considered will of the sovereign—whether monarch, class, or majority of voters— define and secure human liberties, and it must be at once applied to every new sphere in which freedom can act. Although as it brings new classes of men under its sway it plays a radical part, on the whole it is conservative in the finest sense. Though often mechanical it is at its best a chemical entity, continually compounded from the accumulating experience of the race, in the interests of all men, without favor, and based on assertion of the value and dignity of every individual life. Nothing could more completely blur the reality than to think, as some do, of a great half-truth law set over against a great half-truth liberty. Law is a function of the only liberty worthy the name. The two are universally true, and they are mutually dependent and enlivening; but it is liberty at long range and at wholesale that law contemplates, not the prejudice of a powerful party or the caprice of an individual. Likewise, law and order are not to be separated; but this rule applies only where they are both genuine and acceptable to the great majority of those on whom they rest. Order of a sort has often enough been maintained in a defiance of established order so radical as to overthrow all law in the interests of genuine freedom. Through much of the eighteenth century France was as quiet internally as her rulers might have wished, and no people were ever more unruly than the Dutch under the heel of Alva; yet in the one case law was a creature of privilege, and in the other it was battling hard for its integrity.

However, the single underlying basis of modern life that we call law, sometimes set down in writing, but oftener lying only in the back of men's minds, is to be sharply distinguished from the multitude of minute and variable regulations which go by the name of laws. The formulating and recasting of these rules has come to be a business almost wholly political, done—and overdone—by anxious deputies of the people. The maintenance and interpretation of justice is a matter of the greatest delicacy, entrusted to men and machinery receiving the greatest respect. But they also will bear the most careful watching. For neither is the law self-purifying nor does it manufacture the morality it professes. It is a vine of rank growth, and unless we prune and support it to the best of our ability, liberty is apt to be crushed and smothered beneath its weight. The tyranny of law may take root in many places, nowhere more easily than in a lack of social imagination, or in the capture of justice by the vested interests which can best profit through its perversion, or in occasional surrender to popular prejudice and hysteria.

The strangling of law in the ramifications of legislation is an evil of long standing, due to the natural inertia of a ponderous institution, dedicated to an abstract principle and sunk in the immemorial past. It is shown most obviously in the maddening slowness and intricacy of legal forms, which often defeat the very purpose they were intended to serve. Moreover, the seclusion and dignity of the judge, under which the theory of verbal inspiration is maintained, the fetish of precedent, the virtual separation of governmental powers, by which courts are debarred from exercising legislative functions, and their disregard of the best contemporary thought—all have in the past combined to open a gap between the stability of the law and the requirements of the age. Reform can be effective only if the ancient guarantees are continually reinterpreted to meet new conditions and interests, unsuspected when the formulae were first drawn up. Here the letter may often kill, while a wise, far-seeing, and flexible spirit is needed to give life. The gap may perhaps never be closed, but there are encouraging signs that a quiet revolution is under way today which will progressively humanize the content, procedure, and institutions of the law, making them frankly adaptive to the needs of the changing times and, in particular, to the rising spirit of social justice. Like medicine, law begins to turn from the remedying of past abuses to measures of prevision and prevention.

The miscarriage of justice is a catastrophe that can be rendered impossible only in a society thoroughly self-governing in every field and well aware of its responsibilities. The grosser forms of venality are not greatly to be feared: a Jeffreys or a Barnardo cannot often make a scandalous mock of justice in full view of a people furnished with weapons for their overthrow. But there must always be a difficult mean between too immediate and too tortuously indirect control of the judiciary by the people. On the one side lies the subjection of every important decision to a referendum which may express only the whim of an interested majority, and on the other the road is laid open to all sorts of malign influences that can seldom be brought to book. In most countries the changing winds of popular favor have been sedulously avoided, but at the same time it has been made less easy than it should be for the people to discover what forces may be influencing the action of their courts and to lay bare the corruption thus fostered. The covert impress, upon law and upon its interpreters, of a slave-owning caste, of an imperialistic junto, or of the masters of the capitalistic system has been at different times considerable and is not always to be fully withstood. And there is, besides, a more subtle bias to justice in the common tendency, among those classes and professions that have lost their touch with the masses, to develop a general identity of interest with the dominant powers of the day. They come to feel, quite honestly, that the established order must by its very weight have a juster foundation than the attempts to modify or reconstruct it can offer. Jurisprudence takes on, chameleon-like, the color of its own age and moves today in harmony with the politics and economics of giant industry. There can be little doubt that impartiality is often destroyed by this trend, which, however free from conscious favoritism, constitutes a very real and insidious danger. It can be lessened only by demanding in the legal professions, both from within and from without, the highest critical intelligence and the loftiest ethical standards.

The abdication of law in the face of popular passion is a tragedy only too familiar to us in America, with our heresy hunting after the Great War and almost daily reminders in lynchings and mob violence. Owing partly to a lack of confidence in the machinery of justice, these savageries are chiefly a throwback, under stress of deep emotion, to primitive methods of settling differences among men. Hence, they reopen all the old wounds—religious bigotry, race hatred, political prejudice, and class enmity—which centuries of reliance upon law have repeatedly bound up and almost allowed to heal. It is the new barbarians, those half-educated millions, without tradition or the respect for it, crowding on among the engines and institutions of a complex civilization, who, when sufficiently roused, can trample out civil liberty, with or without the acquiescence of the law. And until they can be taught how to take their place in the modern world, we may expect other waves of panic or anger, sweeping over a tolerant people, to make the ancient rights for certain unfortunate individuals or groups a mockery. When this happens, only until the passion wears itself out will the law become again a protector of the weak and the unpopular.

These evils, however, are not beyond our power to correct. Great and often menacing as they are, they cannot keep law from standing as the first bulwark of modern liberty for the individual. The idea of its universal sway and impersonal regard for all men has supplanted most of the medieval allegiances in our present world. It is, beyond question, a permanent part of our inheritance, and if its imperfections and denials can be further removed, we may see the community of the future living securely under a body of law which is a genuine servant of life, respecting no persons yet protecting all. Still more, we may be permitted to hold as our ideal a society lifted to that higher economy of life already attained by a few scattered groups, a society in which the outer trappings of law have all but disappeared and its spirit alone is left to guide and moderate.

CHAPTER III

LIBERTY OF THOUGHT AND EXPRESSION

As the world of Langland passed into the world of Erasmus, it became aware of still larger issues to be met. The great stirring of men's minds that took place in Europe more than four hundred years ago we call the Renaissance—a new birth of the human spirit out of the narrow bounds of authority within which the Middle Ages had confined it. Through two broad channels, religious and secular, the jostling currents of that time are to be traced, channels not always distinct yet widely separated in their origin and in their later course. The Reformation was primarily a religious revolt appealing from pope or council to Scripture, from conformity to personal faith, though its absorption into political rivalries for a time obscured its original character. Secular enlightenment worked through the revival of classic learning, the appreciation of classic art, through new mechanical inventions, a novel theory of wealth, the exploration of lands beyond the ocean, and a dozen other eager impulses to the ideal of humanism, an ideal springing from the attempt of man to reconstitute himself as a reasonable being in an altered world. The two agencies together—the religious and the secular—loosed tremendous forces that swept aside the exclusive tradition of the Roman Church; and the most difficult labor of the new age came to be the creation and assertion of some norm of life that should restore balance to a world robbed of its familiar cosmic philosophy.

From the vantage point of the present we cannot say that either force was destined to succeed. It has become evident what a tragedy was this break-up of Christendom. Since Luther burned the pope's bull at Wittenberg, since Cellini cast his bronze Perseus in Florence and Copernicus hewed down the pillars from the four corners of the earth, the old feeling of unity, that distinctively Middle-Age sense of a single corporate truth binding all life together, has vanished from the earth. And there are few signs, in the multiform society of today, that it is ever likely to be won again. In exchange for this loss and for a good many centuries of blood and bitterness, one clear gain emerges: the right of men to think and believe and express themselves as they see fit in most religious and secular matters—freedom of conscience. The finality and assurance of the medieval world system have faded out of our lives altogether. In their place stands—so far as anything can be said to stand—the enfranchisement of the individual mind. This new possession is of a different sort from the old: it is not a divinely appointed end, but a human and limited means. It is not a perfected social and ecclesiastical order, but a tool placed in our hands, to be used for self-destruction or for world construction. As yet we have hardly decided what to do with this powerful implement.

The church of the earlier Middle Ages was not quite the dark instrument of tyranny which later generations came to paint it. Along with the feudal order, it had half-tamed the barbarian invaders of Europe, and in some countries, such as Anglo-Saxon England, it had virtually re-created the state. But in affairs of internal policy it seldom saw eye to eye with feudalism. Aside from the increasingly narrow rigidity of belief which it enforced, and in spite of all its abuses, the church long stood as a great cosmopolitan society for the defense of the downtrodden and the protection of the common man against the surrounding rapacity. Almost alone it safe-guarded individual rights of life and property from the secular power. Indeed, the dramatic struggles of pope with emperor may be regarded partly as the assertion of these rights in the face of a political system that cared only for corporate security. In the thirteenth century, after a long era of gloom and confusion, something like an equilibrium was established between these two dominions, when each occupied an almost universal acceptance. But with the discovery in civil law of a new basis for personal liberty, one of the great moral superiorities of Catholicism was taken away. As the church gradually relinquished to secular agencies some of its most useful legal and administrative functions, its failings as a religious society stood out in higher relief; and when men began to employ their reason on premises other than those furnished by the church a dangerous precedent was created. When the kings, moreover, found strength enough to command the direct allegiance of all ranks of people within their territories, an unreckoned political weight was thrown into the delicate balance of secular and religious power. Under these influences the authority of the church was bound to be challenged. The same forces that at last put an end to feudalism—the rise of national monarchies, the growth of an intelligent and jealous middle class, and a contagious habit of free inquiry—undermined the ecclesiastical edifice, and a second breach began to widen in the complicated structure of medieval life.

The religious revolution of the fifteen hundreds was long in the making and long foreshadowed. Its crisis came not from above but from the smoldering fires below. Although now leaping into a blaze, now dying back to a feeble glow, the desire for a purer faith and a cleaner polity had never been wholly extinguished. For some of its champions the church had found a place within the fold; others, meeting response from the ignorant Europe of their day, had languished in obscurity; many thousands more, as in northern Italy and southern France and England and Bohemia during the previous three hundred years, were mercilessly crushed for their convictions. But the new learning raised up leaders who could look back with a strange enthusiasm to the early centuries of Christianity; corruption in the church became, or at least seemed, more flagrant than ever before; and unwelcome doctrines and practices were introduced which had had no place in earlier times. As in all the great revolutions, political and economic forces were mingled with the ideals of men, and it is now, perhaps, impossible to disentangle them. This reformation, one of many that had been attempted, swept through to success because it found a growing class of people in northern Europe able to understand its principles, and princes quick enough to profit by its material opportunities.

The courage of a German monk touched off the train, and the forces at his back saw to it, before they were through, that the exclusive power of the old order was broken. Attacks on specific abuses could not fail to end in a general overturning, because the Catholicism confronted by Luther and his followers was seen to be both a tyrant and a fraud by men who had rediscovered the Scriptures and tasted the wine of independent thinking. The ideal 'of the freedom of the Christian man to find access to God in his own way, bound only by the teachings of an inspired Book, was generally replacing the old conformity to the tradition and decrees of the Roman Church.

As an ideal; but unhappily it was not, then or long afterwards, to be realized. In the passion of ecclesiastical and social warfare the first promises of the new spirit were quickly swallowed up. Its betrayers (if that be not too harsh a word) were most notably the same men who had evoked it in the beginning. Private judgment came, in fact, to be little more than the right of a group of resolute iconoclasts to impose their own dogmas and regimen, if they could, on the half-awakened conscience of Europe. For when Luther, siding with the German princes, threw all his new strength into crushing the confused struggle of the peasants toward a religious and social democracy for which he himself had prepared the ground, and when Calvin acquiesced in the burning of Michael Servetus for heresy, it became evident that true toleration, respect for the inconvenient beliefs of others, was as strange an idea to most of the reformers as it had been to the medievalists. Neither in the doctrine nor in the government of their new-won systems were they disposed to yield anything to genuinely free thought. The baiting of Anabaptists and Socinians and, later, of Quakers went forward as furiously with them as did the anathematizing of Antichrist; and their signal victory over the ancient evils came to be almost engulfed in the harsh spiritual pride which was so often a distinguishing mark of Protestantism.

The reversion was all the sadder because it appears to have been inevitable. The temper of the age, as of every age that breaks sharply with the immediate past, was little inclined to a tolerance which, carried out in so unsettled a time, would have quickly led to dangerous anarchy of thought and action. The radicals of that day, some of them anti-formalists whose heirs have been among the most consistent and high-minded of Protestants, raised their voices. To suppress them the leaders were compelled to consolidate the revolution by means that have seemed to many a denial and a surrender of the principles with which it had opened. Liberty of a sort they won—the separate life of certain powerful new sects under armed protection—but no true freedom of conscience for the common man of any nation.

This failure to realize what might have been is one of many witnesses to the degradation of ideals when they are flung into the world and given a space for development. Every movement of revolt that wins some measure of success is threatened with the same tragic cycle—a dogmatism of its own, a hardening of the spiritual arteries, and in the end perhaps a new tyranny as unbearable as the one from which men had once been rescued.

Luther was essentially a type of the "new man," the rebel who, rising from obscurity and challenging the world in unrest, is called upon to control the great forces he has evoked, and who, seeing them slipping from his grasp, must shift his ground and abandon those who might have been his most loyal followers. Insensibly, against his will even, the idealist or the doctrinaire often becomes the opportunist, and a movement is perverted to material ends. In time a new aristocracy, new privilege, and new vested interests take shape, until the grandson of the revolutionist is apt to confront his own generation as a sentimental stand-patter.

And so, like the church of the early centuries, Protestantism largely abandoned the sort of man and the type of mind which gave it its beginning. Both this earlier church and Protestantism were at first radical movements, dedicated to the establishment of a new personal and social Kingdom among men. The books of the New Testament reveal themselves to this end as the most incendiary of all literature; but since respectability and power have come to the church it has been used only too often to bolster the *status quo* and to attempt the repression of questioning men. For as life itself must be continually tearing down and building anew the body it inhabits, so the spirit of truth can be preserved only by making over with every generation those institutions in which it becomes incorporated. Reformation is not a single achievement but a perpetual process. Few things are more pathetic than a man or a society resting on the laurels of the past, blind to the truth that victories are lost when they are not being eternally re-won.

The most appealing figure of this time is Erasmus. The understanding and sympathy of our own day reach back to him as to few other leaders of that century. Incapable by temperament of taking sides in a partisan quarrel, he was fated to be deeply involved in its issues and to be continually and violently misunderstood. His was the kind of nature which at its worst belongs to the merest trimmer, but which at its best may serve the highest ends of tolerance. It may see farther to right and left than any other and hold its own temperate ground with a firmness perforce concealed in irony or wit. A devoted humanist, Erasmus belongs to the second and critical phase of the Renaissance, in which it was necessary to use new powers as weapons of defense against the rising despotisms of doctrine and ecclesiastical polity. There is tragedy in his death at the moment when the Protestant revolt was sweeping down to the Mediterranean and the forces of Catholic reaction were girding themselves to thrust it back toward the North Sea. Between these antagonists his life was crushed out. The real adversaries of this time are not Luther against Pope Leo, or even Calvin against Loyola, but all of them together against Erasmus and the broad disposition of reason and liberalism of which he was the most constant exemplar.

Not for more than a hundred years afterwards was that temper to win through. Even Milton, who stood at the beginning of a new epoch of history, died before freedom of religious belief received in the revocation of the Edict of Nantes its last crushing blow at the hands of the old order; while the Camisards, later still, succumbed in southern France to the same holy war that had all but wiped out their ancestors, the Albigenses, half a millennium before. During the century and a half of war and persecution that devastated western Europe toleration was often submerged altogether;

yet in the end neither Jesuits nor Inquisition, Cameronians nor Salem witch-baiters could prevent its long-delayed coming. The Socinians had from the first extended it to their fellow Protestants; Roger Williams set up the first wholly secular state, tiny though it was, in the wilderness of Narragansett; the Catholics followed in Maryland and the Quakers in Pennsylvania; Chillingworth, Milton, and Jeremy Taylor championed the cause, and England enjoyed under Cromwell and again under William of Orange a limited liberty in religion; Frederick II made Prussia the first tolerant state on the continent. Through the later sixteen hundreds a new spirit was in the air, and as they drew to a close John Locke set forth a practical philosophy of toleration, won from Protestantism at its best, which became a gospel for the succeeding generations. And so conviction by force gradually ceased to be the dominant issue of two continents. Official crusades against heterodoxy weakened, faltered, and in most places were allowed quietly to lapse, though the civil and educational disabilities of nonconformity existed until long afterwards in those nations maintaining an established church. Men found themselves released from a false duty and a self-imposed fear; and conscience began slowly to take its place with law among the ministers of personal liberty.

Religious freedom, wherever since then it has been fully won and maintained, rests on a twofold policy of governmental toleration. The first step in this process is the granting to all individuals the right to hold their favorite religious or non-religious opinions, and to all groups the right to worship as they please, subject only to respect for the civil rights of others and the keeping of the peace. The second step (which by no means always inevitably follows) is the placing of all sects and their members on a complete legal equality, by refusing to levy a general tax for the support of an official state church or to allow its members any special privileges within the state. In either case freedom in religion becomes a department of civil liberty, maintained in its integrity and restrained from excesses by national laws. Never more secure in any one country, therefore, than the whole fabric of civil rights, in our own day religious freedom depends ultimately, as these civil rights do, on political action. Certain memorable clauses in the constitutions of the American states and federal union gave this new freedom its first and most impressive salute from government.

As we look back on these troubled decades it seems to us that the reformed churches were very slow in learning the one great lesson of polity which, more than anything else, brought about their intellectual emancipation. Except among the following of a few obscure men, freedom from the old secular entanglements was a long time in being realized. The radical Covenanters of Scotland who took arms in the attempt to impose the rule of general assembly and synod on the southern kingdom belonged to no free body, nor would they acknowledge the rights of their neighbors to religious or political institutions of any different sort. Conformity by force ran along with conviction by force and has been a principle hardly less vicious in its application. Until the government of the church willingly drew apart—or was set apart—from the state, and until the field of ecclesiastical law came to be completely marked off from that of civil law, the Reformation was unable to realize its better spirit. To the states, as well, separation proved an unmixed good; for their own reformation, which belongs to a later time, could not have been worked out on right lines while religious and political affairs were still interwoven. Certain sects are still officially recognized and supported in countries where they have long been prevalent, but there is no thought of compulsory adherence: the old pre-

sumption of *cuius regio eius religio* has fallen into the desue-
tude it deserved. Establishment is now little more than a
name, and it is generally true that bodies under governmental
sanction have less vitality and hold a narrower place in the
life of the people than those which have broken away. Church
and state have learned that they are distinct in function and
purpose and can best live with mutual respect and the least
possible measure of formal contact.

Unhappily, this is one of the forgotten lessons that must be
learned again and again. There are always groups and sometimes whole peoples willing to use the church for political
purposes, or the state for ecclesiastical purposes, to gain some
temporary advantage of their own. Today we can witness
side by side in North America an early and a late stage in
the travail of religious liberty. The long alliance in Mexico
between church and state corrupted both these agencies,
and the present attempts to separate them indicate the same
bitterness and varying success which have elsewhere marked
the course of that process. Our own country has been from
the beginning professedly a secular nation, in which the larger
principles of this question have been, we may hope, settled
for good; yet (for example) during the Great War many
churches became little else than bureaus of national propaganda and morals, and since the war powerful sectarian
organizations have repeatedly tried to dictate to the federal
and state governments policies of a religious or semi-religious
character. Religious freedom guaranteed by public opinion is
a good deal more difficult of achievement than religious freedom laid down in constitution or statute, and like civil liberty,
it is never wholly safe from waves of popular passion or
prejudices that may, while they last, undo the laborious work
of centuries. The state, we say, must defend itself at all cost,
yet not at the cost of violating the deepest convictions of its

citizens; for, if millions of people could be found today resolute in refusal to let their churches become mere adjuncts to the civil power in time of war, the state would be compelled to respect their position or go down in revolution. The church, we say likewise, has a compelling social mission in the world, but not a political mission. It stands on higher ground and looks to farther and larger ends than the state can ever do; and any future attempts to confuse the functions of the two can end only, as all previous attempts since the Middle Ages have ended, in degradation and disaster.

As a result of this independence the church, at its best, has again been able to devote itself to its own spiritual and personal aims. Dedicated to those truths which are the essence of its Founder's teaching, it acts directly on the individual himself, knowing that it can thus most effectively inject its teaching into the center of every sphere, religious and profane alike. It has gladly abandoned the older claims to temporal sovereignty and the newer claims to alliance, open or covert, with secular power, so that it may be free to assert once more the supreme importance of the spiritual life. The Kingdom envisaged by the church has nothing to do with pope, prince, or parliament. It is never more difficult to look steadily toward that goal than when church leaders are enmeshed in the banality and intrigue of another world. Moreover, partly through this reabsorption into the purer life of religion and partly through the freshening influence of secular free thought, the nineteenth and twentieth centuries have witnessed a quiet revolution in Protestant belief, no less radical than the violent revolution of the sixteenth century. We are still too close to the event to catch its whole meaning, but it would seem that the church is in process of exchanging the authority of the Bible for the authority of the individual conscience fortified by knowledge and experience of every sort. And rising over this new foundation, an edifice even loftier than the old is in process of construction.

We have said that freedom of conscience was won; but more truly it came about through sheer weariness and a change of front on the part of both opponents. Its victory in the later seventeenth and the eighteenth centuries was more apparent than real. Europe had become sick unto death with the passions roused in the long years of warfare. Persecution on a wide scale ended not because those in authority surrendered to an abstract principle, but because they found it useless to fight any longer. Religious revolt had been dignified into an open warfare, in which lines of conviction were drawn with such force that a further appeal to arms only strengthened their power over men's hearts, and it seemed prudent, if not necessary through exhaustion, to call a truce. Tolerance thus became in a sense inevitable because intolerance had so signally failed.

This armistice was partly the effect, but still more the cause, of an alignment of forces, then taking shape, which shifted the center of gravity in public affairs. Religious belief and adherence were gradually ceasing to be the most important facts in a man's relation to his world. A new orientation of thought, political rather than ecclesiastical, had begun, and energies were turned in a very different direction. On the one hand, the sort of man who, in the sixteenth century, had led the revolt against abuses in religion, was becoming aware, during the eighteenth century, of flagrant abuses in government; and on the other hand, those men to whom heresy appears always as the worst of crimes discovered that heresy promised to be more dangerous along the new lines than along the old. This latter class included a good many who were Protestants as well as the great majority of Catholics. For Protestantism, no longer itself a heresy, had become

merged into a new European equilibrium not to be upset
without a good deal of disorder and confiscation. The unsuccessful rebel seems a martyr to the few and a traitor to the
many, but with success he sooner or later finds a settled place
in the social order; he becomes for the old enemies who were
unable to suppress him an obnoxious ally, a power to come
to terms with and employ if possible for the overthrow of
future rebellions. Thenceforth privilege belonged in part to
those insurgents who had won to power, and many of them
developed a community of interest with the older forms of
privilege in the maintenance of social stability. Political ideas
which were to shake the world in another era, being without
a tradition of sentiment or achievement, were regarded by the
older and the newer oligarchs alike as indefensible nuisances
ruthlessly to be stamped out.

* * *

The religious enlightenment, the course of which we have
traced, shows only one side of the shield. Along with it, sometimes touching but oftener breaking away to follow a path
of its own, runs a passion for freedom of thought and expression, conceived as a broad principle of all civilized life,
rather than as an adjunct merely of the church. The story of
this development has to do, not with open warfare or with
national strategies, but with single men of genius. Their
books or public lives, flung into the maelstrom of the later
Renaissance, became powerful influences in transforming a
society of mental conformity or confusion into one which was
on the road to alert and independent thinking. The reformer
Zwingli may claim a part in it, the moderate theologian Erasmus, and the radical theologian Socinus. It got itself expressed
in literature and the arts by Montaigne and Shakespeare,
Michaelangelo and Rembrandt; in philosophy by Spinoza,
Descartes, Bayle, and Locke; in natural science by Leonardo

da Vinci, Bruno (the most illustrious of its martyrs), Galileo, and Bacon; in political theory by Hooker, Grotius, Milton, Harrington, and Montesquieu. As a practical ideal of conduct it has often been given expression, nowhere more notably than by Voltaire, who wrote: "Though I disagree with every word you say, I will defend with my life your right to say it."

Fostered by such men as these and by their followers, a wholly fresh spirit of intellectual integrity and self-reliance came into being. Reason began to be taken frankly for the guide of life. A disinterested love of truth for its own sake gradually permeated the social fabric until, with the eighteenth century, something like a genuine public opinion, confident and critical, appeared in western Europe and North America, broadening the Renaissance into a new phase of enlightenment with a new type of leader. Scepticism and rationalism—in the older, wider sense of those terms not limited to antireligious thinking—became common attitudes among the upper ranks of society and then filtered slowly and unevenly into the increasingly powerful middle class. They brought with them the progressive secularization of life—a development bitterly resisted by the old church and the reactionary Protestantism which leaned on bibliolatry and the temporal power of the clergy, but welcomed alike by those who wanted pure religion stripped of its heavy baggage, and by those who were tending toward a naturalistic philosophy presumed to have outgrown all religion whatsoever. Magic, witchcraft, the cheaply miraculous, all the tattered finery that ignorance and credulity throw about questions of aesthetics, morals, or exact science, had to be stripped off and cast aside. It was necessary, as well, to contend with all those forces of privilege which battened on the old ways of thinking, and with the natural inertia of the human mind, which, though it may sometimes be a saving grace, is oftener one of the most exasperating stupidities of man.

Thenceforward free thought was to be the sharpest weapon in the armory of progress. By its aid, civil liberties won or acknowledged in an earlier time, were reaffirmed and enlarged under new conditions. By its aid, political liberty, then about to enter on its great century of achievement, was gained. Only by its aid can the struggle for industrial freedom in which we find ourselves today be brought through to success. But the most striking triumph of the new spirit is to be found in the development of science. One of the landmarks of the modern world was the publication, in 1543, of Copernicus' *De Revolutionibus Orbium Coelestium,* which began a three-hundred-years' duel between truth and prejudice officially ended only when the book was dropped from the papal index in 1828, although even since then an occasional village has voted that the earth is flat! Astronomy was thus the first of the new disciplines to fall foul of theology and habit, but it was far from the last. Few important discoveries or inventions based upon observation and experiment have since then gone unchallenged by these same forces; yet no sound scientific principle has in the end failed to make its way. The great geological war—now safely ended, one hopes—was a vivid memory to our grandfathers, while the last echoes of the battle of biology, fainter than our fathers heard them, still reverberate intermittently about us. The future of natural science, at least, is assured, if only because of the technical and industrial triumphs for which it is responsible. Yet when science, as it sometimes does, also grows intolerant and objects to any dissent from its dogmas, it too must be resisted no less resolutely than any other tyranny of the mind. Free thought, long the champion of science, must when confronted with scientific despotism shift its own ground in order to remain loyal to the spirit of truth.

The soldiers in this war for the liberation of humanity, as Heine called them, had also to create and get accepted the machinery for expressing and preserving free thought. Here it was neither popular crusades nor great books which carried the day, but a species of guerrilla fighting, innumerable skirmishes here and there—by no means ended yet—for those rights of speech, of assemblage, of teaching, and of the press which we count among the most precious guarantees of liberty. Since they were first affirmed these rights have been declared and denied, won and lost and re-won a thousand times, in different places and in the interest of different causes. Written now, most of them, into national constitutions and statutes, they are determined largely as civil or political questions, since freedom of expression is limited only by the prohibition to violate the law, and the law is a more or less obedient creature of the popular will. The securing of them, in so far as they have been secured, is a splendid enough chapter of practical statesmanship, worth rereading occasionally for encouragement in hours of darkness.

These rights found one parent in the religious revolution and their other in the rebirth of humanism. They hark back in spirit, therefore, to that more distant day when humanism first flowered in a little pug-nosed philosopher addicted to button-holing his fellow citizens on the dusty street corners of ancient Athens. It was the serene *Apology* of Socrates which first announced the principle of free speech and its two primary purposes: to liberate the individual conscience and to educate the social body. These purposes are still as valid as on the day they were explained, with patient irony, to the five hundred turbulent judges who sent their author to his death. For only through unhampered discussion and criticism can be satisfied the need of a man to express his hard-won convictions and the equal need of society to learn the truths by which it lives. These needs ought to be identical, or at least compatible, since men in the mass have no other way of knowing and choosing the right than by listening with open minds to what every one of their more articulate fellows has to say. Nor is it sensible to choke off the apparently dishonest or unintelligent: who can decide surely whether a man is dishonest or unintelligent until he has had a hearing? Yet clearly in this frail world the two needs, personal and social, do not always dovetail. The individual is only too apt to use the dynamite of intellectual freedom without due regard to its devastating possibilities. This is only to say that man is of necessity far more conservative than men. But out of this conflict rises the perennial problem, faced everywhere since complete repression was given up as a bad job: how to balance public security with the search for truth, how to give the spoken and written word enough freedom to do all possible good, without endangering the society which harbors it.

The problem has been met, we say, by toleration. But we should understand that toleration is not fixed; it must trim its sails to meet the changing winds of social values, slackening here and pulling up there. As the clearest observers have always seen, it is only qualified freedom, since it presupposes an outside authority which has permitted expression and hence can limit or even prohibit it at will. And in point of fact, toleration has been succeeded by complete lack of restraint only in those fields of thought which no longer matter very much except to the individual, and which do not promise too great disturbance to the social structure. We speak pretty much as we please about religion, because the issues of religion do not move the world as they once did; we are more careful when it comes to politics and still more cautious concerning the present economic order. A man may say there is no God or (in some places) that there should be no dictators, but he is likely to get into trouble if he suggests that a match be put to the constitution or that all wealth be turned back to the proletariat who created it. And if, in war time, he is thought to imperil the safety of the state by spoken or written word, his right to free expression is most drastically denied. Even a democratic society will not surrender its coercive powers until the subject of discussion has passed, for that society, into a purely academic realm.

This means, in effect, that there must always be a license of speech which is liberty carried to dangerous lengths. Toleration, with the censorship it implies, will be necessary as long as we have government or social control of any sort over the individual. The question becomes one of fixing this control within bounds permitting the greatest possible measure of personal liberty compatible with social preservation. Bernard Shaw, assuredly not in alliance with the interests, has here spoken with his usual intelligence and frankness in the preface to *Saint Joan*. Toleration, he says, is continually rising and falling through a scale that marks the strain under which society maintains its cohesion. A line must be drawn somewhere between allowable expression and what is judged insanity or crime, in spite of the risk of mistaking sages for lunatics and saviors for blasphemers. "We must persecute even to the death; and all we can do to mitigate the danger of persecution is, first, to be very careful what we persecute, and second, to bear in mind that unless there is a large liberty to shock conventional people, and a well-informed sense of the value of originality, individuality, and eccentricity, the result will be apparent stagnation covering a repression of revolutionary forces which will eventually explode with extravagant and probably destructive violence." Or as Macaulay more dramatically put the matter: "Let your demagogues lead crowds lest they lead armies; let them bluster, lest they massacre; a little turbulence is, as it were, the rainbow of the state; it shows indeed that there has been a passing shower, but it is a pledge that there shall be no deluge."

Yet we must not too readily assume an inherent conflict between personal liberty and social control. The purpose of state coercion, in other fields as well as in this, is primarily to override individual coercion, and such activities as are restrained by law should first seem clearly to hinder the freedom of other individuals as well as that of the community at large. Rightly used, compulsion is never brought to bear against a man except in the greater interest of another man or in the equal or greater interest of a group of men. Conversely, every act of personal liberty cannot but rest on a corresponding act of social control; for, if all of us were allowed to do as we pleased it is obvious that no one could do anything he pleased. In a genuinely organic society, the body can act as a whole only in and through harmoniously acting members; and likewise, the health of each member is dependent on the efficient functioning of all other parts of the organism.

Liberty of thought is not, therefore, to be measured by such specific subjects of discussion as are at any moment wholly unrestricted or widely tolerated. New follies and heresies will spring up in place of the old, and prejudice can no doubt run as bitterly today as it ever did. Our true success lies in keeping free and using all the available channels of communication and information—those agencies of personal rights and independent thinking—which must gradually educate the world to breadth and wisdom. So considered, freedom of conscience has been one of the greatest of modern achievements. For it has meant permanent release, not of a physical thing like life itself, nor of a chemical entity like the law, but of a moral faculty whose first great discrimination—in matters of religion —was only a prelude to its later triumphs. As law is in the best sense conservative, so is conscience radical: it can cut to the heart of prejudice and sham and raise every man to high distinction as the arbiter of all human values. The two move side by side, one supplementing the other in the life of a rational individual or community. If intellectual freedom has immensely increased the scope of man's activities, it has also widened his responsibility to mean that every decision must be made under the influence of this freedom, and no blunder or crime committed for lack of it may be excused. Of later years it has often enough been silenced and repressed and frightened half out of its wits, but it seems impossible that it shall ever be lost. In every crisis of history, whatever the issue of the hour, independence of belief and expression must be gained before any real settlement can begin. Official heresy-hunting is perhaps less indulged in than of old, but the great organs for the control of public opinion—schools, churches, newspapers, political platforms—can on occasion be falsely used by the forces of fear, habit, or privilege, to vitiate the ideas of great masses of people and to suppress their aspirations. Yet it is a losing game, because the western world has at last learned the unique value of intellectual freedom, and men are always ready somewhere to rise to its defense.

So liberty of conscience, won and honored in the struggles of the past, is eternally challenged and has eternally to be won again. We cannot say it is ever more secure, except as its aid in the gaining of new victories reveals it increasingly essential in civilized life. It is always hateful to the oligarchs, old and new, whether they depend on the reasoned allegiance or the affection and sentiment of men, because clearer and freer thinking endangers their control. Such liberty can be degraded to serve as a mere stepping-stone to power, only to be flung away when it has served its purpose; but it can also be guarded as a flaming sword flashing at need to rid the world of the tyrant.

CHAPTER IV

LIBERTY AND GOVERNMENT

The Renaissance and the long wars of religion were not to be carried through without far-reaching effects on the political life of their time. They led, in fact, to two new conceptions of the state that entered before long into bitter rivalry. During the Middle Ages there had been in western Europe no great self-conscious nations such as we take for granted today. The theory was that of two supreme powers, the temporal and the spiritual, standing shoulder to shoulder, complementary in scope and purpose; but in practice Cæsar and Peter were constantly encroaching on each other, and the empire, by no means a universal system, was often only one loose feudal hierarchy among many. So far as secular sovereignty was a fact it fell to the stronger barons, who laid down the law and governed their fiefs with little restraint. Emperor and kings were not so much national rulers as ultimate landlords, from whom titles could be legally held. Decentralization, carried to its farthest limits, had all but obliterated the puissant state of Augustus and Charlemagne.

When this elaborate feudal edifice began to crumble, its judicial and political activities were taken over in each country by the one man who could represent the emerging nation as a whole. Society began to split apart into the sharply distinguished elements of king and commons, and the functions of the great medieval corporations were divided between the state and the new self-assertive individual. From among these functions, the monarch gathered into his own hands the powers of law and government. As a result of this involution the people secured the protection of a single unified body of law administered by trained jurists; and the kings consolidated what political strength had belonged to the baronage, the clergy, and the remnants of ancient popular assemblies into a few great systems of personal despotism. The same social and economic forces which freed the serfs turned the old domestic tenant classes into one subject body, a "people," with national sentiments and allegiance to a new master. In many respects the lot of the common man was improved, yet apart from certain legal rights his liberty was still sacrificed almost completely to government. He had merely exchanged a petty tyrant for one powerful ruler who thought more about the glory of his kingdom than about the aspirations of its meaner inhabitants.

The communes of northern Italy, though lying on the high-road between Germany and Rome, were nevertheless the most conspicuous areas in Europe in which the medieval idea had never gained a hold. Adventurers had been playing there for a good while with independent power, and it was in one of these city-states that, at the height of the Renaissance, Machiavelli put forth a theory of political range and functions, a practical manual of statecraft and polity, which fitted the rising temper of the time and, directly or indirectly, was caught up as a gospel of the new monarchy. His book, *Il Principe*, was inspired by the career of one neighboring despot and dedicated to another, but the Prince has been Henry VIII or Philip II or Peter of Russia or Richelieu or any other politician who has spent his life in perfecting the system of absolutism. The center of that system was the half-forgotten assumption that sovereignty and the state are identical and are embodied in the person of the reigning monarch. During the conflicts in which the temporal pretensions of the church were discredited and the old nobility weakened, this idea developed rapidly, and at various times there emerged over most of the continent a new type of secular political power, well integrated, ambitious, and internally oppressive, based on the divine right and the moral irresponsibility of kings. France was long the most notable of these, but Austria, Spain, Russia, for a time England, and later Prussia were among them, as well as a host of smaller principalities that fell short of their models only in strength and extent of territory.

The inevitable revolt was not long delayed. The new monarchies were in fact undermined by an extension of the very enlightenment which had made them possible. The same intelligence and self-reliance which enabled a few powerful men to build up the great despotisms led in the end, when it had permeated the whole body politic, to their overthrow. First caught up and used by the kings for their own ends, the spirit of nationalism became in the hearts of a long-suffering people the strongest of those forces which were one day to give them control of the state. Two incendiary ideas—natural law and popular sovereignty—were revived out of the past to become fuel for the intellectual revolution preceding the great armed revolutions.

The conception of a majestic law of nature as an invisible censor standing behind man-made statutes or compacts and silently proclaiming all men to be equal in their rights and duties, had had a long and ancient medieval history. In the modern world Melancthon, Hooker, Grotius, Milton, Locke, Montesquieu, and von Wolff form a brilliant apostolic succession of thinkers who bridge the three hundred years separating Cesare Borgia and Thomas Jefferson as leaders of men. To this idea of equality the ultimate authority of the people in government came as a practical corollary. Running back through two lines to the Roman republic and to the free Teutonic nations, it was never wholly lost sight of, even by pope or emperor; but the attempts of Arnold of Brescia, Rienzi, and Etienne Marcel to realize it amid the ignorant and fickle societies of their days ended inevitably in tragic failure. The English political writers of the seventeenth century gave it a new impetus—Harrington came out boldly with "King People," the protagonist of his democratic romance *Oceana*—and discussed most of the practical forms with which it was afterwards to be invested. The two ideas were blended, and the hard fact of despotism explained at the same time, in the social contract theory of Hobbes, Locke, and Rousseau, according to which the free people, before the beginnings of written history, had agreed with their chosen leaders to exchange the liberty of self-government for protection and security. Hobbes used the social contract to uphold the principle of autocracy, but in the hands of his successors it appeared as an extremely bad bargain which the people had every right to revoke by resuming their original power. Natural law and primitive compact have now gone the way of other ingenious fancies, and events were to prove that Hobbes was writing for the past and Locke and Rousseau for the exciting future.

The revolutions came also through the extension into the political sphere of such partial liberties as had elsewhere been won. When men began to think about government as they were already thinking about literature and art and science, about law and religion, and set about drawing analogies from the latter two, the years of despotism were numbered. Civil liberty seemed perpetually in danger and in fact of little worth in itself, before a political authority over which the subject had no control. Only by bringing government under the law, as relations between man and man were already being brought, and by basing public law, as private law had in the end to be based, on the enlightened approval of all those whom it affected, could personal liberty be extended and made secure.

But perhaps the most powerful impulse to freedom came out of the reformed churches. The right of revolt followed

naturally from the conviction that obedience to God stood
before loyalty to any earthly potentate or institution. The
Lutheran and Anglican churches, it is true, adapted themselves to the forms and sometimes to the reality of irresponsible power. But Calvinism was essentially an aristocratic
system which demanded that authority be delegated from
below rather than imposed from above; and the Independents,
rejecting the interposition of popes, bishops, and presbyters
alike, rested full power directly in the congregation. Applied
to society as a whole, as these polities inevitably were, they
largely determined the three forms in which the spirit of
freedom was to clothe its political victories: the constitutional
monarchy, the representative republic, and the pure democracy. For while the doctrines of the Reformation sometimes
led to new tyrannies over mind and action, the administration
of its churches had an immense influence in the new political
era. As Lowell said, Puritanism, believing itself quick with
the seed of religious liberty, laid, without knowing it, the
eggs of free government.

The Dutch and English commonwealths, first of the great
struggles against the tide of despotism, mark a period of
transition between two epochs of very different character.
Though the religious issue was still dominant in the world,
these countries looked none too certainly toward a future
concerned mainly with secular politics. Milton's life was spent
in the divided service of two ideals—freedom of belief and
freedom of government—and he lived to see the first cause
all but won and the second all but lost. The same dual interest
was faced by Cromwell, although he is remembered as a
champion less of political liberty than of religious moderation.
Under his rule a greater measure of toleration was probably
enjoyed than at any other time and in any other country since
the beginning of the religious wars. But his armed domination

of parliaments, his taxation by ordinance, his confiscation of local charters, and his scourging of Ireland are rightly considered the acts of a tyrant, no less arbitrary and far more determined than King Charles. In a sense the Protector deserted one cause, as many of the reformers before him had deserted another, sweeping to power on the crest of a rebellion whose better principles he was compelled to repudiate in the name of social order. Hating anarchy more than despotism, he was forced reluctantly to choose between them. Cromwell never succeeded in setting up popular institutions, and there were true patriots who recoiled from his administration as bitterly as from Strafford's "Thorough." The pathos of his career lies in the continued frustration, by the men and conditions about him, of his sincere efforts at some beginning of representative government.

Because he failed in his larger purposes, thirty years afterwards the work had to be done again. The keenest memory of the Commonwealth to the men of the following generation was its swamping of political rights by military power; and when William of Orange was called in, the future ascendancy of the civil arm was guaranteed. The Petition of Right in 1628 had been the first great statement of free public law; the Bill of Rights in 1689 at last set the authority of Parliament above that of the king. There and thereafter was begun a constitutional government which has withstood the fearful corruption of early party life, the shock of the American revolt, twenty-five years of the French Revolution and its aftermath, and all the convulsions of the nineteenth and early twentieth centuries. Its later development, from the rule of a jealous aristocracy to a system delicately responsive to the popular will, has been fairly steady and not spectacular: a business of roll calls rather than of street barricades. British political liberty is perhaps the securest and remains the most adaptable in the world.

It was in America, however, that the English civil war found its logical and radical conclusion. A hundred and fifty years after Pym and Hampden had fallen, a body of young colonials whom they would have hailed as comrades completed their work. The importance of the American Revolution in the history of freedom is threefold. It was the first purely political and economic upheaval, uncomplicated by questions of religion. It set up a wholly new type of state— the federal republic—which was to show the possibility of popular government over wide areas and on a grand scale. And through written constitutions reserving to the individual certain fundamental rights which not even a state committed to universal suffrage could override, it demanded that the government become the avowed protector and no longer the enemy of civil liberties. The Declaration of Independence stood in reality nearer the end of the Revolution than its beginning. For half a dozen generations the stubborn individualism of the frontier had been gnawing away at the breast of British imperial policy. When the rope at last snapped, well pondered political theories and free local institutions were already at work. The decade and a half following Bunker Hill fixed the larger outlines of the new order, and the republic which was to endure into the twentieth century with astonishingly little change of form was well under way.

The continent of Europe was prepared for neither the English nor the American method in liberty. Most of the eighteenth century, the period between the wars of religion and the wars of patriotism, showed despots—enlightened but still despots—on the thrones and an ominous quietness about them. The old fires had burned themselves out, and the new were not yet ready to be lighted. But beneath the surface their materials were being assembled; a still submerged middle class was becoming slowly and painfully introduced to the doctrines of political and social liberty. In France the old regime danced most carelessly on the rim of the smouldering volcano. Through the long reigns of two of the most impressive of monarchs, among the cynical philosophies, the debased polity, and the wars of dynastic ambition which were their outward insignia, the forces of change were rising from below to the great moment of expression. The figures of Montesquieu, Voltaire, Rousseau, the Encyclopedists, and the vivid example of America became the chief teachers of the nations. As John Morley has well said, it was through the mockery of Voltaire that the free, critical genius of the Reformation, late and changed, made its decisive entry into France. His task was to spread abroad the nature and authority of common sense; Rousseau's was to point out the great gulf fixed between privilege and the ordinary man. And when a half-awakened people was confronted with the hapless combination of a diamond necklace, an unmanageable debt, and a miscast locksmith and dairymaid upon the throne, only a small spark was required to touch off the charge.

With the explosion, not only government but every accepted element of the social order was thrown into solution. Old civil disabilities, old religious oppressions, old and new administrative tyrannies—all the survivals and recrudescences of the feudal spirit—went under, and for a while the first principles of law and religion and government as well. With a completeness never before (and only once since) realized in modern times, the institutions and allegiances of the past were obliterated. Yet destruction was never justified, even by the demagogue Danton or the cold fanatic Robespierre, as more than a clearing of the earth for future growth. Society had to be rebuilt from the bottom, and the work of those revolutionists remains of fascinating if tragic interest because of the ideals that were always struggling to create from the wreckage of civilization a new world for which the time was not yet ripe.

In this great drama Napoleon is the adventurer, the strong man who appropriated the forces of change to personal ambition. "I am the Revolution!" he said; and "I have slain the Revolution!" The Jacobin and the emperor are one person; the fiery, lean successor of Robespierre sees fit in time to take for his consort an archduchess of Austria and Holy Rome. The France of ninety-three passed, in the hands of a calculating artillery officer, into a France as strange to the stormers of the Bastille as it would have been to the builders of that fortress, and almost as subversive. Napoleon succeeded where moderate and radical reformers alike had failed, by fusing the passions of his day into a unity, by setting before the nation a prospect that for a while seemed more splendid than either legitimacy or the cancellation of the social contract. His military empire, with its contemptuous affectation of the old and covert betrayal of the new, meant, says H. G. Wells, a waste of the largest opportunity for rebuilding a shattered society that has come to a man in modern times. But the failure was probably inevitable. Like Luther, Napoleon was compelled to desert the more liberal influences that had helped him to power, and like Cromwell, he strove vainly to establish his regime on some firmer basis than arms and popular enthusiasm. Far more shamelessly than either of them he perverted the deeper strivings for liberty that had made possible the Revolution itself, but his position was no less inescapable than theirs: he was not a master but a creature of destiny, and his absolute rule seemed to most men the only alternative to the Bourbons or another corrupt Directory.

Yet though political liberty went by the board, rights of other sorts were conserved through the empire and maintained in the darker days of the restoration. Napoleon accepted the imperial crown from the Roman vicar, but he did not and could not bring back ecclesiastical domination over men's minds; and Louis XVIII could set up again the *fleurs de lys* but not the feudal hierarchy of France. Although personal monarchy returned, because there had been no historic preparation for sovereignty of the people, equality flourished under it, and a genuine national fraternity of spirit. Legal privilege, the burdensome agrarian system, religious disabilities, most restrictions on free speech vanished for ever, and a new jurisprudence, new taxation, the rise of the peasant farmers and a commercial middle class, and *la carriere ouverte aux talents* gave promise that the old bondage was never again to be imposed on the nation.

Most illuminating of all, the revolutionary idea survived and has been spread abroad through Europe by the French armies. Not only were institutions remodeled, but popular feeling, long asleep, was awakened; distant Serbia in 1804 inaugurated the struggles for national union and independence that were to crowd the annals of the nineteenth century. Political history for a hundred years was in large part an alternate ebb and flow succeeding the first momentous wave. The figures of Metternich and Bismarck personify the forces of absolutism that fought bitterly every new attempt to wrest their restored privilege from them; but the tide was not to be stemmed. Germany and Spain had turned against the tyranny of Napoleon; Bolivar and San Martin in America were the first to pierce the gloom which settled down with the restoration; Greece flared out against the former enemy of all Europe. After fifteen years of Bourbon rule France asserted herself once more, and led by a veteran of Valmy, who walked to his throne draped in the tricolor, gained by a precarious compromise the first liberal government on the continent. Two years later a third English revolution was sealed with an historic roll call in St. Stephen's. With another generation grown to manhood fresh fires broke out. The spring and summer of '48 saw half the capitals of Europe behind barricades, witnessed new democracies and new repressions, and when the smoke had cleared away much of the old tyranny remained only as dying embers in the ashes of the past.

Another thirty years again altered the aspect of affairs. France merged herself into the main stream of progress after the nation had been humbled by a foreign conqueror and the first of the new sans-culottes had fired the capital. In this country, after the Jeffersonian and Jacksonian revolutions had set popular government in motion, four years of war on an unprecedented scale determined that national unity was to prevail over the rule of a landed aristocracy founded on chattel slavery. Britain completed her reformation in two later bills that set up a genuinely democratic franchise. Through a combination of propaganda, diplomacy, and audacious guerrilla fighting, Mazzini, Cavour, and Garibaldi brilliantly swung Italy into the family of nations. Only in Russia was autocracy keeping a firm hold on a people scarcely yet infected with the revolutionary fever; while in Germany an empire on the Napoleonic model was offering wealth and pride as substitutes for liberty, and Austria was still managing to divide and rule her turbulent subject peoples. There and on the fringes of western civilization—in Ireland, in Turkey, and among the great peoples of Asia—the struggles for free government were yet to come. But elsewhere the passion for the popular control of the state, so notably (if far from completely) satisfied, began to cool, becoming less and less a prime factor in the movement of events; and men's attentions were turned oftener to problems of another sort. This was the beginning of the end of a great political era.

The position of the German peoples in this stirring age was unusual. The impact of Napoleonic France fell heavily on their deliberate civilization, still shaken by its vivid memories of the devastation of the Thirty Years' War and the restless energy of Frederick II. Jena and Auerstadt admitted the revolutionary ideas, but the rulers learned only to distrust their own subjects and to adopt the strategy of the soldier of fortune who had turned aside the revolution. Germany and Austria, in the hands of their two resolute ministers, achieved new unity and power, not as in Italy by a wave of patriotism rising from below, but at the expense and by the direct suppression of popular feeling. The masters of central Europe caught eagerly at the chance to impose personal monarchy such as England and France and Spain had for a time endured and then cast off. That this latter-day imperialism became possible was due in great part to the alternating excesses and timidity of democracy in the half-century following the Congress of Vienna: the liberal forces had developed neither the poise nor the resolution capable of standing against the assaults of the old order when they were delivered intelligently and in good earnest. A powerful army was to be the engine of destiny, and there were to be no more slaughters of Leipsic or sacks of Magdeburg on native soil. Germany was to rise by strong government at home and by wars abroad. Her common people and the neighboring states were to pay the price.

This philosophy found its logical outcome, after sixty years of swift material prosperity, in the Great War. With the opening months of the conflict came a frenzy of imperialism, the apotheosis of irresponsible power, in its closing days catastrophe, revulsion, and the assertion of the long denied spirit of liberty. With her princes in exile and men of the people in the seats of power, Germany found herself standing somewhat in the position of England in 1689 and of France in 1830 and again more securely in 1871—ready to attempt a constitutional regime gauged to the political temper and experience of her people. The trial of popular government coming at a time of momentous change on all sides, its life has been menaced by forces of economic unrest which the English revolution was unaware of, and which during the French revolutions were just beginning to gather strength. Whatever the event, this is a stage in the progress of free government which most of the western nations seem destined to pass through.

Russia's career has been still more striking. Until well into the nineteenth century she was to outward view a type of the Renaissance state which Machiavelli had contemplated; but beneath the surface lay a tremendous agglomeration of medieval communities, held together by the old conceptions of universal church and universal empire. Her public character came from the feverish labors of Peter and Catherine, her true nature from centuries of isolation and preoccupation with the central fact of the land. When she was at last forced to rouse herself, her change, perhaps more apparent than real, was rapid. In less than fifty years the serfs became legal freemen, an industrial society was superimposed on the ancient agrarian life, the forms of constitutional government were granted, and all the complicated problems of the modern state appeared. Yet a jealous oligarchy still held the reins of power, and its bitter oppression added fuel to the revolutionary flames burning in the minds of those alert to the events of history elsewhere. Since the great peasant heart of the people still belonged to the Middle Ages, the explosion, when it inevitably came, was as elemental and all-destroying as the French Revolution. Autocracy crumbled at the first set-off, and underneath was revealed an emptiness few had foreseen. As in France, the people had had no historic preparation for responsibility, and there was no moderation in taking or in using it. Her brief essay at democracy was pushed aside with contempt, and in the hands of a few resolute doctrinaires Russia leaped at a bound across the four hundred years of struggle for civil and religious and political liberties which had made and remade the nations of the West. She disregarded all of them to plunge into the experiment of an entirely different sort of society, based on principles scarcely older than the men who were adopting them. It is more than a little strange, this poverty and this arrogance, the apparent willingness of Russia to do without so much that the rest of us have thought essential, and her confidence in salvation by an inverted despotism of manual workers. It is possible that genuine freedom may somehow be coaxed in time out of the present dispensation; and it is possible that, like France again, she will fall into reaction and find herself once more at the foot of the ladder.

In Japan, striding confidently to the forefront of world power and influence, the movement has been only less swift. When Perry sailed into the harbor of Yokohama, Japan even more than Russia exemplified the medieval state projected strangely into the heart of the modern world. Her revolution, fourteen years afterwards, comprehended the work of long eras elsewhere. Centralization of power, abolition of caste, conscription for military service, freedom of occupation, confiscation of the great estates and their leasing to a new oligarchy of wealth, religious tolerance, universal education, the cabinet system of government—all these are familiar marks of our own civilization. Secured in less than a decade, they seem to have transformed almost overnight a fourteenth-century society into a nineteenth-century society, and Japan has since run with the greatest nations in Western lines of development. She has for the first time caused democracy to be regarded as other than the privilege of the white race; and yet imperial Germany is perhaps her most constant model. Her future is a speculation of no slight interest. Will there be a quiet progress toward a genuinely liberal form of government? Is she to go through the highest peak of Prussian imperialism via an aggressive war and its possible collapse? Or have her changes been, like Russia's, too sweeping to carry the great masses of people along with them, and may she therefore find sudden pause in a convulsion that will throw her whole life into temporary chaos? We know little enough of her mind and the forces acting upon it.

Behind these great struggles of the last century and a half have lain the two doctrines we call democracy and national- ism: that is to say, the ultimate control of government by majorities and the popular worship of the democratic state. They are the first articles of our political faith, and here in America until the other day they went unquestioned; yet neither of them, held uncritically, solves the ever-recurring problem of freedom, which is the balancing of personal and communal rights. In themselves they will not take us very far toward this reconciliation of individual liberty with social control. Thought and its expression are, as we have seen, primarily a man's private concern, but the abuse of expression must come under some restraint by society. Government is by its nature social, and unless the liberties of the citizen are care- fully safeguarded they may easily be swamped by the ma- chinery of the state, on whatever authority it acts. Under the old monarchies such activities as the subject shared in were matters of tolerance, concessions granted by rulers who could without much trouble take them away. Yet when political practice was reversed and government became the creature of the people instead of their master, it was not transformed at once into the obedient servant of each one of them. For just as the Protestant Reformation led to the independence of certain self-governing sects without bringing about freedom of conscience, so the triumph of the democratic state does not necessarily insure personal immunity from its arbitrary acts. Hence there are, in the winning of full political freedom, two stages. The first consists in subjecting the legislative and executive powers to the ultimate control of the people; the second consists in protecting the individual and the minorities from the new leviathan released by the majority. Every free constitution needs, like our own, its first ten amendments, and a perpetual guerrilla warfare must be fought to keep them alive.

Thus democracy, or the sovereignty of the people as a whole, is by no means identical with their liberty as individuals. In the first flush of revolution, personal freedom has sometimes enjoyed a brief glory, but the inescapable trend of government toward social control rather than social expression soon makes itself felt. The anarchist would solve the problem by doing away altogether with the state, in which, even at its best, he can see only latent tyranny. Yet human association must go on, and most of us think today that in its political form it can be made to serve and enlarge human freedom and happiness. It must necessarily do so in a positive and not merely in a negative way. The old agrarian liberalism of Jefferson, which could flourish only when every man had a homestead to support him and a wilderness at his back to escape into, has gone forever. Where the frontier once stretched there stands now an industrialized, highly complex society turned in upon itself. No nation can freely leave the weak and unfortunate to be crushed by its wheels. In such a society, paradoxically enough, true personal freedom for the common man without resources of wealth or talent is often to be conserved only through a broad policy of social welfare. The newer liberalism demands not a restriction but an extension of government. It demands that the state concern itself with the practical problems of the good life as well as with narrowly political functions, that health and education and decent living conditions and equality of opportunity shall be made the heritage of every citizen as much as the right to vote and hold office and sue in the courts. Only in this way can human rights, in the largest sense, be protected from the overgrown power of property and private organization.

There are of course grave evils in the functioning of democracy. Majorities may be ignorant, capricious, and intolerant; well-organized minorities may push to the limit whatever selfish power they can grasp; party machines in the hands of professional bosses may form a vicious *imperium in imperio;* elected officials may betray their trust. These things have always been with us; but there are other problems peculiar to the new trend toward the socialized state. Bureaucrats may easily become dangerous nuisances, and experts in high places ridiculous pedants. Legislation like our own child labor laws and income taxes is resented by many as infringements of a salutary freedom to contract or to be secure in private property; and such restrictive measures as the eighteenth amendment and the sterilization of defectives are held to be violations of still more elementary personal rights. These laws and others similar, which are transforming our whole way of life today, are means of increased social control, it is true; whatever human value they possess lies in the extent to which they increase social and individual expression along other lines or for a much larger number of people. For we are here on the meeting ground of civil and political life, where the two are often indistinguishable from each other. And the criterion of liberty in both fields must be the golden mean between unrestricted personal freedom and the public interest. The scales during most of the nineteenth century were tipped low in favor of the assertive individual; today they are perhaps inclining too far on the side of the social mass. Ultimately the balance is to be maintained by political action, and the private citizen, however complex and technical the specific issues of politics may become in the future, must remain the arbiter of the broader policies on which they rest. Above everything, he must remember in all humility that he does not exist for society and the state, but society and the state exist for him.

The actual method of guarding personal liberties from the intolerance or sheer weight of popular government has always been a difficult problem. The Greek and Roman republics hardly recognizing this, the life of the citizen was therefore almost completely surrendered to the state. Nowhere throughout modern Europe has it in theory been well solved. The executive is subjected to the legislature, more or less popularly elected, yet until the end of its term the legislature itself is legally accountable to no one. Acts of the British Parliament are the supreme law of the land, and where written constitutions exist the people's representatives may amend or annul them without reference to other authority. But one of America's greatest contributions to political science in proclaiming the rights of man was to safeguard them by carrying responsibility one step further. The fundamental law is embodied in a constitution which not only limits the powers of government and which cannot be altered by Congress alone, but reserves a well-defined sphere of activity as a basic right of the citizen; and an independent judiciary holds the final power of interpretation. Thus there is created a scheme of immunity from arbitrary acts of the executive and, paradoxical though it seems, from illegal laws passed by the legislature. The courts have been made the last guardians of freedom. Oppressed minorities or persecuted individuals should be able to turn to them for redress and unless the very life of the state is at stake find protection in the exercise of their political and civil rights.

Yet as a matter of practice personal liberty is little more secure here than elsewhere. It has been sometimes a good deal less secure. The Briton who relies on a Parliament theoretically knowing no master, but in practice deferring rather anxiously to custom and the popular will, may come off better than the American who looks to a federal court which tests statute law by the Constitution yet which is far removed from the hearts of the people. For what can be explained may be explained away, and while the courts are less likely than the legislature to deny, as a result of popular clamor, the rights of an individual or a minority, the very conservatism of the judiciary and its insensibility to changing conditions often blind it to the continual necessity for reinterpreting the terms of personal liberty in the face of governmental encroachments or apathy. The truth is there can be no system proof against stupidity or design or the natural working of institutions. There is no document, however solemn, whose meaning cannot be twisted, and no political machinery that cannot be thrown out of gear. Reliance must be placed at bottom on an alert, vigorous, and liberal public opinion, determined to bring the interests of the state and of its individual members into closer and closer harmony and able to impress its own purposes on both of them. To provide for expression of the popular will by the universal secret ballot is only half the battle; the other half consists in keeping open channels for the free formation and education of rational convictions and in rallying the forces of intelligence and kindness and generosity to the attack on prejudice and ignorance and ill will. The forms of democracy are futile without its spirit, but an active capacity for self-government will make its way in spite of poor tools and numerous enemies. Only where such a public opinion thrives can there be true freedom under democracy. This power of the democratic state to deny liberty is immensely increased by the modern religion of nationalism. The great revolutions of the eighteenth and nineteenth centuries brought patriotic fervor back to the world after the long eclipse that had lasted, with a few meteoric breaks like those under Rienzi and Joan of Arc, since the fall of the ancient republics. The state, released at last from the hold of universal empire, feudalism, the church, and selfish despots, drew to itself all the scattered allegiances of earlier times. It became at once the creature and the master of the people, the latest of the gods that man has always been creating in his own image. Despite its immense usefulness, it is, like a Homeric divinity, not altogether manageable. The people to be free must be served by the laws and protection of an autonomous state, but the state to be free must fight for its life amid a world of ambitious equals who own no moderating authority. The medieval federation and subordination of powers has been replaced by a convention called international law, which hangs only on mutual convenience and may be discarded at the call of any more insistent interests. There is thus opened a yawning gulf between national liberty and the true political liberty which consists in the control of government by the citizens in their own interests. A country's freedom has been almost of necessity linked with the strength of its government, and since power is most readily gained by aggressive war, we have the spectacle of humane peoples believing themselves compelled to invade the basic rights of other peoples in order to maintain their own. Foreign relations have been the last function of government to hold out against the democratic spirit: retaining the old unprincipled methods of secrecy and cunning, their policy is often twisted out of all resemblance to the genuine sentiment of the nation. Here is nothing less than patriotism degraded into a vice, the recrudescence of barbarism in a false guise, and the vitiating of the popular temper, which speaks unmistakably for peace whenever it is not betrayed into the necessity of fighting.

Moreover, in its extremity the spirit of nationalism, born of revolution, may destroy that civil freedom of the individual on which it ultimately rests. Worship of the state, carried today to as fierce heights as ever the worship of the church or of chivalric honor was borne in days past, cannot but be in perpetual conflict with the elemental rights of the citizen. In a society feverishly preparing for war or more feverishly engaged in war, with its conscripted armies, its mad suspicions, and its complete distortion of normal values, immunity from the arbitrary acts of government becomes a mockery; and when peace comes, which is often more devastating than war, the damage to individual liberty cannot easily be restored. The whole truculent spirit of Fascism, as it has raised its head in Italy and half a dozen other countries including our own, is threatening today the temporary eclipse of personal freedom behind a new screen of national and racial prejudice.

The road away from these perils of democracy and nationalism is a long one. What first steps we need to take are clear and have often enough been pointed out to us: universal education, a more alert and well-informed public opinion, the willingness of the best men to undertake responsibility at the polls and in office, and perhaps such devices for better expressing the will of the people as proportional representation and referenda on vital questions of national policy. But behind these reforms will have to come a sweeping reconstruction of our basic political ideas. There are encouraging signs that such a reconstruction is even now under way. From the time of Plato men have once in a while questioned the value of the contemporary state as a permanent vehicle of civilization. In our own day not a few are asking whether through the doctrines of democracy and nationalism, as we have practised them, the fullest aspirations of man for liberty can be realized. And some of them have ventured in answer to suggest how freedom may come more completely into its own.

The understanding of what lies back of our present way of political life will help us to see what may possibly and profitably come out of it. For the state that we, have known is, as a community of interest, an evolved and no doubt an intermediate stage in the history of human association. It has had a beginning and is not likely to be without an end. The earliest type of community, rising directly out of the family, was the clan, an exclusive caste organization based on real or assumed kinship and allowing a large measure of local autonomy. Among peoples on the fringes of civilization the clan has persisted to modern times; as the medieval system of manor and fief it won to a compromise with another tradition; and in the monastery, the guild, and the secret society its genius formed and still sometimes forms little islands in the stream of an alien culture. The true state, founded on the principle of authority instead of relationship, does not appear until later. Ancient Assyria and modern France, different in so many respects, are alike in their emphasis on military and civil obedience, whether it be rendered to a tigerish despot or to an amiable abstraction known as the people. The states began, so far as we can judge, with the beating down of the clans into a vast dead level of slavery. They were first founded and preserved by leaders in war, who gradually became keepers of internal peace, dispensers of justice, and thorough administrators. At length, by a more or less complete inversion of power, they were dispossessed by their former helots. Yet the democracies which thus at length emerged did not abolish authority: they merely transferred it. The people rule, and ability is purchased in the open market, but we have seen that the modern state still bears heavily on groups, individuals, and foreign nations who do not fall in with the views of its momentary majorities. Obedience by force, however narrowed or euphemized, remains the foundation of the state.

This is not the mark of a genuinely self-controlled society. Somehow a larger degree of liberty must be squared with security, efficiency, and justice in government. And here is room for the third type of human association, only now beginning to be recognized as possible, which may be called the partnership. That is a wholly self-determined, voluntary community in which co-operative action has taken the place of both kinship and authority as a social bond and function. It means, in the widest sense, government equally by and for the people in their every individual and social relation. And, in order to be at all effective, it must be world-wide, or at least world-powerful, in scope. It is hard to see how it can be brought to pass internally without a devolution and distribution of many political functions, a broadening of duties and responsibilities that will result in every citizen's becoming vitally concerned, through vigorous local bodies, in the conditions of his own and his neighbor's welfare. Externally, it becomes a problem in balancing local self-determination with government on a planetary scale, in formulating and applying laws between the nations at least as equitably as they have been formulated and applied between individuals within those nations. Hence the old greedy and irresponsible state will have to part with many of its dearest powers, relinquishing some of them to the smaller communities of which it is made up, and others to whatever league or court or association of peoples is entrusted with the administration of affairs affecting all countries alike. The magnitude of this double task, the overcoming of passion and prejudice and the forging of a new political morality—for a continuous act of social faith must underlie the mechanics of it—is immense. It means pushing to a conclusion the great struggle for complete, but now only half-won self-expression in government. It will make all of us citizens alike of our own neighborhood and of the world.

In the end the craving for liberty will determine the type of institutions under which man will choose to live. Up to the present the nationalistic state has been the surest repository of freedom; but just as former stages have been passed over and their virtues incorporated into the body of civilization, so we may look to the rise of other world forces to shift the center of progress, and with it the dominant loyalties of men, to fields that will better serve the ends of liberty. For one thing, the society of the future is likely to be a good deal more than partnership in our accustomed ways of government. Of old the clan presided over the whole round of existence; and though religion has been recognized definitely as a personal affair, industrial life no less than political may come again to be a function of the community. But that, as we shall see, is another matter.

CHAPTER V.

LIBERTY AND WORK

There is a legend that on a memorable eighteenth of June, forty years after Richard Arkwright was granted his patent for the construction of the improved spinning-jenny, a Jewish money-lender stood on a mound in Flanders watching the cavalry of Napoleon fling itself for the last time against the allied host. Late in the afternoon he had seen the battle lost and won, and as the French army fell back to its long retreat he left the field hurriedly. A relay of good horses to the coast, a fast sloop, and horses again carried him into London early on the morning of the twentieth. Fresh and confident, he appeared on 'Change within the hour and quietly bought to the limit of his ability. When the great news of Waterloo reached the city, British stocks, which had been depressed on the report of Blucher's defeat two days before, soared to new heights, and Nathan Rothschild emerged as one of the wealthiest commoners in Europe.

Here, at the catastrophe of one of the most brilliant episodes in history, was marked dramatically the beginning of an epoch whose opulent triumphs were to outshine the destiny of armies and empire. Arkwright and Watt and Whitney have made possible Manchester and Essen and Pittsburgh, and they in turn created the great masters of industry and finance, of whom the Rothschilds were the forerunners, and who have gathered powers of startling magnitude into their hands. We know well enough—for it is still being re-enacted about us—the course of the revolution these eighteenth-century inventors so quietly inaugurated. The center of gravity in modern life has been shifted from the villages to the city, from simple domestic crafts to intricate and costly machinery in great factories, from statesmen and soldiers to the men who own and use money. Increased control of wealth through credit and interest, and the speeding up of production by mechanical means wiped out in a few decades the immemorial system of home industry. The workman can no longer own his tools, as he had done previously since the dawn of history, but he and his fellows have become dependent on a large-scale employer for them and for the conditions under which their work is carried on. We call this, in capitals, the Industrial Revolution, but it has been a social revolution as well, altering almost every condition of ordinary life and giving a different mental outlook to people of every class. In range of interests it has been far more extensive than any purely political movement of the same period, for it touches, as no mere change in government could possibly do, men's pocketbooks, their intimate lives, and the disposition of their waking hours.

The Industrial Revolution was the work of no one class or generation of men; it has swung, in fact, largely beyond direct human control. When the medieval economy of manor, guild, and petty itinerant trader gradually merged into the Renaissance, a new sort of mind and new sorts of institutions were formed to carry on the world's work. In a society dominated by the church and conceived to be, as a whole, subject to the moral principles of Christianity, mutual obligation of service stood at the base of economic as of all social life, and usury, profiteering, hoarding, and the exaltation of property over living were declared sinful. This unity of life Protestantism boldly shattered, erecting in its place a dualism under which secular and religious affairs could be carried on in parallel but exclusive territories, with very different laws, standards of conduct, and spiritual sanctions. Salvation became solely an individual concern, while in lay matters the once-denounced acquisitive ambitions of men were allowed free play. High profits and great property came to be regarded as the marks of diligence, the taking of interest a rightful use of money, and poverty something of a disgrace.

To meet the new opportunities thus offered, economic life was reorganized on the capitalistic basis that we know today, with its avowed goal the wealth of the few instead of the functional interrelation of the many. The typical unit of business became the corporation, which could undertake permanent enterprises, command the joint resources of its stockholding members, and yet limit their liability in case of loss. Commerce was transformed by merchant adventurers who sought out distant markets and materials, at first in great monopolistic companies controlled by government (for statesmen had come to see the national value of trade) but afterwards under free competition and resentful of state interference. Banking grew up to provide for the constant use and fluidity of capital, and the idea of credit for its wide extension. With the decline of the guilds, industry fell into the hands of larger employers who could have no personal interest in their workmen's lives, and in England successive enclosures of farming land created a growing class of dispossessed laborers. The actual operations of spinning and weaving, potting and smithing and cabinet-making, were still carried on in village cottages or in small shops, owing to the lack of tools for large-scale production. But when, in the days of the American and French struggles for free government, machinery was devised to simplify and accelerate the processes of textile manufacture, when steam power began to be applied to manufacture and later to transportation, the flood gates of another era were thrown open. Work and workers were quickly drawn into the cities, production leaped upward to the confusion of once stable prices and wages and living costs, and a strange new life of urban miseries and excitements sprang suddenly into being for millions of industrial serfs and thousands of industrial barons. First in England and then in every Western nation the smoke-grimed factory rose as the symbol and strength of the machine age.

The swift rise and supremacy of the powers dominating this revolution coincide with the shift of human interests from things political to things industrial. As the first consideration of a man's life became for a while not his professed religious belief but the sort of government he lived under, so again it has veered from government to his daily labor. The forces of the age are more and more impressing upon man that he is no longer importantly a churchman and no longer exclusively a citizen but above all a worker, a creature of the industrial machine that is striving to satisfy the rapacious demands of present-day life and to stimulate them when they are not rapacious enough. The movement has been a complicated one: it comprehends steam and electricity, coal and oil, cotton and steel and rubber, and all the physical contrivances of the last hundred and fifty years that make the mechanism of our living as different from Benjamin Franklin's as his was from Archimedes'. Its central fact is the application of science to the arts of manufacture and to commerce and the growing worship of these as the surest vehicles, if not perhaps the ideal ends, of progress. The combination of unfettered business enterprise, technology, and machine industry with a ruthless philosophy of self-interest has created a Great Society like nothing the world has ever before seen. Adam Smith is its prophet, its religion a thoroughgoing individualism, and its dominant motive the making of goods primarily for gain and only incidentally for use. Most men depend for their livelihood on the efficient functioning of this society, and a very much smaller number are able to use it as a means of acquiring wealth and power. Life having become, as we say, predominantly economic in character, it is increasingly clear that industrial factors are largely determining and will continue to determine the course of history.

Those few men who are distinguished as being the masters of this altered scene we call capitalists, because they can control the accumulated products of industry. They have become the inheritors of those irresponsible powers over men's lives which in other days belonged to the barons, the ecclesiastics, the kings, and the great statesmen. The idea of monarchy, barred in turn from civil, religious, and political fields, has broken through as confidently as ever in industry, and our captains of business and finance are as truly tyrants, in the Greek sense, as the Medici or the Mathers were in their own age and in their own way. For the great convulsions of the last hundred and fifty years in government were far from abolishing the natural despot: they merely persuaded him to yield ground along one line and turn his talents to the acquisition of power along another. The autocratic spirit growing up under the Industrial Revolution and overshadowing economic life in the nineteenth century had nothing in common with the principles of free government that were developing at the same time. Yet democracy, flushed with its triumphs over the old regime, made little protest against this new tide of privilege. Just as the kings of the Renaissance could build up systems of absolutism while granting many civil liberties to their subjects, so the capitalists found a denial of economic freedom possible at the same time that political freedom was being won. Under modern industry conditions were brought about not to be controlled by the ballot.

As the heir of such tremendous power, the great capitalist holds a position that should be by its very nature a defensive one. He is a member of the newest aristocracy, not of birth nor of martial prowess but of wealth, by virtue of the general belief that money is the most worthwhile thing in the world and the ability to acquire it the most respectable human faculty. His strength lies in the genuine achievements, past and present, of the system he heads and in the striving of other men for position and privilege like his own; his seemingly fatal weakness is in the historic inability of aristocrats to use irresponsible power for the common good. He is the lineal successor of rulers who, in spite of many virtues and because of one besetting vice, have been condemned and deposed as exploiters of their fellows. The strength of the capitalist is relatively new, but the clear verdicts of history against his forerunners should afford him little confidence in his ability to stand permanently against the spirit of freedom. The feudal, the ecclesiastical, and the political castes have all risen to meet the needs of their hour, have all slowly lost popular support through perversion of trust, and have all been discarded as incidents—major incidents—in the march of progress. Capitalism has developed the spirit of enterprise, organized men and materials for production on an immense scale, created untold wealth and widespread comfort, and encouraged a good deal of foresight and co-operation among men. Controlled as it is by an open class, unstable in individual membership, it is nevertheless assured a large measure of natural ability by the glittering prizes it dangles before young men of ambition and talent. But also capitalism "has caused waste almost without limit; it has rewarded injustice and dishonesty; it has promoted a standard of value that sacrifices manhood to merchandise; it has marred some lives with pride and luxury, and many more with want and joyless labor; it encourages in human nature all that is hard, combative, unscrupulous, and hinders the development of finer qualities." Whether or not the system can withstand the stigma of these manifold evils remains to be seen. If it cannot, the class whose fortunes are bound up with it must go to the wall.

As Germany was for a long time the type of feudal organization, and France of political despotism, so it may be considered that in the United States the modern capitalistic society has reached its peak. The Western world, discovered when feudalism was already a thing of the past, was being settled during the period of religious dissension, but its independent nations arose in the high tide of political revolt at the very beginning of the quiet and promising revolution in industry and mechanics. Hence although the United States has escaped the older struggles for freedom, the results of them have been incorporated almost as a matter of course in our fundamental law. Whatever breadth and tolerance much of American life has had is the result of its distance from the bitter factional struggles of Europe and its consequent reluctance to recognize the existence of hostile classes in the community as any European people is forced to recognize it. But *The Wealth of Nations* was born in the same year as the Declaration of Independence, and the economic society it envisaged found here a task worthy of its best efforts. A new people with eyes fixed mainly on the facts of environment; a national realm of almost unbelievable wealth in raw material and the means of manufacture; quick communication with the markets of the world; the absence of a nobility or a stolid peasant class; immense energies unencumbered with fear of neighbors or serious complications of race and religion; freedom of choice in occupation; a vast supply of labor—all are inevitable factors in the rise of our capitalistic system, perhaps the only agency that could have made of the United States the great nation it is.

It was not until the last third of the nineteenth century, after the destruction of the agricultural aristocracy of the

South by the joint efforts of northern business men and free farmers, that industrial capitalism took the helm. And not until then was the machine age far enough advanced in this country solidly to support the new system. But since the eighteen-sixties, popular government and plutocratic industry have, as in no other nation, here marched hand in hand. For a good while the fundamental impossibility of reconciling them went unrecognized, and even after it was seen, the sanity and strength of national democracy was able to counteract many of the vicious and wasteful tendencies of the industrial system. The early horrors of English factory life were not repeated, and until the other day there was always the frontier to escape to. Yet capitalism soon became an *imperium in imperio* which sometimes overshadowed the political structure and at all times has injected itself more or less covertly into political affairs in the attempt to mold them to its own purposes. The names of Gould and Morgan and Rockefeller have during the past seventy-five years been more revered in America and their personalities have left a stronger imprint upon the country than those of Garfield or McKinley or Harding; and politicians, faithfully adjusting tariffs and taxation and currency systems to serve the needs of manufacturers and financiers, have refrained from more than half-hearted interference with industry's vaulting ambitions. The meaning of this power of big business over government—the extent to which wealth within the commonwealth promotes or hinders the good life for the humbler citizens of the republic —has become one of the most ardent questions of our recent history. Certainly few other governments have been so closely identified with the spirit of capitalism, and none other runs a greater danger of being altogether confounded with it.

This is one side of the shield; Samuel Gompers and the Third International (let us say) show the other. Protest and revolt have been as inevitable as in other fields of autocratic control; and they have taken, of necessity, a collective form. In all the rich diversity of the labor movement there appear to be three broad types of theory and action. The first two are dependent on the trade unions, those altered successors of the guilds which, though their legal existence is hardly a century old, have become powerful spokesmen and champions of the workers of the world. In this country most of the unions are content to accept the capitalistic system as inevitable, seeking within it to obtain for labor every possible advantage of the sort enjoyed by the employer. Chiefly by strikes and threats of strikes which are kept as far as possible within the law, they fight directly for full recognition, higher wages, shorter hours, better conditions of work, perhaps for a share in local shop management. Indirectly they lobby among the major political parties and support those candidates for office who can secure specific legislation in their favor. Though their strikes and demands are often of the same nature as these, the British unions have further committed themselves, along with other forces, to a complete political program through a national party of their own. With a policy on every major issue confronting the country, the Labor Party looks toward the gradual and constitutional replacement of the present order by a politico-economic system based on complete government by and for the people and to the just reward of labor—called social democracy, evolutionary socialism, state capitalism, and half a dozen other similar names.

Besides these two wings of the movement, one conservative in methods and aims, the other conservative in methods but radical in aims, there stands a third, frankly revolutionary in both. Contemptuous of political action and fiercely class-conscious, it resorts to violence when there is any chance for success and would erect over the ruins of private property and the democratic state a communistic society ruled by a minority of the workers for the good of the whole class. The first impulse toward this "scientific socialism" came from Germany. In our own day it has come to partial realization on a vast scale in Russia. An epoch-making pamphlet flung out from Brussels into the turbulence of 1848 became the first popular statement of the new faith to be followed by the laborious treatise which received such startling fulfillment in another generation. Before Marx there had been Fourier and Robert Owen and the Oneida Community and a dozen others, groping among theories and experiments for some social truth in the midst of ravening individualism. As closet philosophers and as little isolated groups of peaceful if peculiar workers, these earlier communities could be ignored or debated on the highest grounds; but as a militant counter-system to the elaborate middle class way of life, Bolshevism, cutting through to the material interest of millions of civilized men, has become a battlefield of passion and prejudice around the very fundamentals of political and social life, around property rights and the rule of industry.

Thus the later nineteenth century and the first years of the twentieth have, apart from their concern with the narrower issues of politics, run more and more clearly along two divergent lines. On the one side were the opening up of larger fields of industry, the wider circulation of capital, the exciting race for new markets, the nearer correlation of government to the demands of economic power. On the other side were the restlessness and sporadic revolts of the workers upon whose labor economic power is largely maintained, and their more insistent demands for a larger share in, and control over, the wealth they did so much to create. The main currents of life flowed smoothly enough through constantly increasing ease and prosperity; the undertow, once in a while disturbing the surface, was swift with questionings and swelling bitterness. Our Great Society was neither so beneficent nor so solidly based as its spokesmen with such confidence declared.

Into this drama broke the World War. Yet overwhelming as it was in almost every department of life, the war stands here only as an incident, an interlude, among the play of forces more significant than itself. Although the conflict was caused largely by an ambitious capitalism and its horror has become a powerful argument for restraint of capitalistic forces, the war itself scarcely modified the essentials of the struggle. We remember well enough how the declaration of war seemed to repeal economic laws; how the lions and the lambs of labor and capital lay down for a few months together; how an emergency state socialism came into being in an hour. But we remember still better how, with the armistice, our unparalleled coherence and singleness of purpose were shattered; how the state gave up most of its uncomfortable responsibility, and how the old rivalry was resumed with greater intensity than ever. Meanwhile the cataclysm in Russia had broken on a startled world, to become an inspiration to some, a warning to others, anathema itself to others still, but an event destined to exert a profound influence on future events in every country.

So the conflict was thrown again into solution, in a world far less stable and complicated with a thousand motives and actions. It is the leading fact in our savage society today, lawless in many respects but in none more alarmingly so than in the industrial warfare everywhere being waged about us. Ours is a society of tremendous outbreaks, of tremendous suppressions, of violence often preferred to reasoned adjustment, of spies and *provocateurs,* of "settlements" that are mere breathing spaces between battles, of a public that pays, no matter whose the victory of the moment. One is reminded of the civil wars of Rome during the last years of the republic, when a passionate extra-legal field of conflict—serving as the arena of a political absolutism—without tradition or precedent to govern it and hence outside the influence of the spirit of the law, existed within the state and widely affected the lives and interests of the people. This cannot be called a breakdown of civilization; it is rather a change from one sort of civilization to another. In our own day it becomes a stern warning to all the integrating forces of modern life to swing the industrial struggle into the control of law and subject it to the liberating influences that society has learned to use in civil and religious and political strife.

That this warning will in the fullness of time be heeded is confidently believed by those who have faith in the ability of man to direct his own destiny. What we call socialism, as any one of a score of formulae or practical systems, may be full of errors and extravagances and very human selfishness. But socialism in its larger sense, as the newest and justest appeal for the rights of the many against the privilege of the few, for self-determination and equality of opportunity in the face of vested interest, is in process of becoming a lever that will move the world. Although there has never been an age without an economic struggle between the masses and the classes, this struggle until our own day was always overlaid and confused with other important questions. Only now, in a swift, compact society that has half-settled, and is in course of forgetting, the great religious and political issues of the past, does the economic conflict stand fully revealed as the first concern of man. Its older phases were agrarian, largely unconcerned with the processes of government: the peasants asked for little else than relief from their galling, superimposed burdens; the landed aristocracy were content with a system which allowed their ambitions free play. The newer battles are industrial: both the workers of the modern world (sometimes in combination with the farmers) and the capitalists of money and merchandise have learned that the state can be used actively to promote their own interests. The result may be, and sometimes is, selfish government wholly by one class, as the only alternative to selfish government by another, since, carried to their farthest and narrowest length, such policies lead to a Bolshevist or a Fascist state. There is, however, a third more agreeable possibility, to which the course of events in the past has given us a clue. For while the rule of capitalism has shown no signs of avoiding the abuses of the older oligarchies, the power of labor, which at its widest takes in all but a tiny fraction of the social body and at its best holds the vision of a free world, may well bring about in the end a genuinely socialized economic order, one that will repeat in another sphere the benefits which elsewhere have flowed from the democratic way of life.

Historically, therefore, so far as we can now see, the industrial unrest of these latter days has marked the opening of another chapter in the long struggle for liberty. As a subject man has won his release from custom and personal law; as a churchman, from superstition and clerical domination; as a citizen, from the tyranny of monarchs and political systems; and now, as a producer of goods, man is feeling his way to the mastery of the industrial machine as his ancestors mastered the repressive conditions of their environment. This truth in the welter of our antagonisms has lifted the struggle to an historic plane. The battle is not of necessity between laborer and man of wealth, or between trade union and trust—not even, in the last resort, between soviet and parliament. It is joined between the powers that act for freedom and the powers that act for bondage. The continuity of their opposition holds through centuries of changing terms. And as we view in perspective the course of like action and reaction it is difficult to doubt that the end here will be as it has been before, that out of many stumblings and strayings will come in time freedom of work and control by the ordinary man over all the conditions of industrial life. We are still on the upward sweep of the movement. The great crises, elsewhere than in Russia, are ahead. We are likely to see changes as vast in the economic structure of society as the nineteenth century produced in the political. The struggles of today seem at the same stage as the national and democratic struggles after the French Revolution: the first elemental explosion has taken place, and its effects will long influence the balance of world forces. We need not expect the ruthless communism of Moscow in 1919 to become the final solution of the future, any more than the rabid mobocracy of France under the Terror became a model for the modern state; nor may we look for much help to the nibbling tactics of the "conservative" trade unions, which too often merely extend to a lower level and to a limited class of workers the harshest and least imaginative traits of capitalism. When it at length arrives, industrial democracy will take a variety of forms, but it will be a far freer thing than communism, and far more thoroughgoing than trade-unionism. It will, one may foresee, bear marks of political democracy, the most conspicuous of which is the diffusion of practical sovereignty. There are many others, necessarily including equality of opportunity, the production of goods for use, the elimination of waste, the equitable distribution of wealth, protection from injustice in high places, and the chance for artistic expression in craftsmanship. But self-government is its most vital function. These other things will prove to be by-products of every individual worker's realization that he is a responsible member of the economic order, that on his shoulders falls a fitting share of the burden and the benefit of the world's labor. He will have become the free citizen of another commonwealth.

Whatever the event, we shall all have a stake in it. No intelligent man, unless he withdraw from practical life altogether, can be apathetic or consciously neutral. In the older conflicts for liberty there could be some detachment: the artisan might feel himself unconcerned with the swaying fortunes of the religious wars, the frontiersman indifferent to the political revolutions at his back. But every human being plays some part (though not always a part easily classified) in the complexity of economic life. He is both producer and consumer of goods, worker or executive or capitalist or any combination of these. The material interests of all men are directly engaged; every incident in the long conflict is in some way brought home to the daily life of the whole world. And every incident ought to be viewed in relation to the historic movement of which it is a part. The meanest strike or lockout is more than an isolated skirmish for a few dollars' higher or lower pay; it is one more blow on the wedge that is cleaving society apart, an intensifier of the vicious class distinction and class hatred beginning with the building of factories and tenements and leading, in one extreme direction, to the Russian Cheka and its results. To determine the ultimate responsibility for such things should be made the first business of the whole people.

For even if every man is directly concerned in the struggle, he need not become a rabid partisan on either side. The pacifist, as an acute observer has recently said, can be a conscientious objector to the strike and its repression much more safely and easily than to war. Sympathizing with the cause of labor as a whole and looking to its final victory, he may nevertheless regard any particular outbreak as futile, costly, wrong, and a pitiful denial of civilization. In the end the great issues are to be solved, as in the international field, by a substitution of law for warfare, a law which for the good of society at large will forbid certain destructive activities of both contestants and will enlarge other more truly liberating activities.

The end of it all, we say, will be the democratic principle in work. But capitalism has no idea of surrendering on demand. It can exert the vast strength of inertia and on occasion deliver tremendous frontal attacks against its enemies. On the defensive, and sometimes shaken, it finds an attractive refuge in palliatives and evasions. Yet philanthropy and organized welfare work in industry, for whatever purpose undertaken, are in themselves of small service in tempering the deeper causes of unrest, and in the end usually create more contempt than goodwill, because they destroy the self-respect of men who are demanding not veiled charity but open justice. Nor can wars, even though dressed out as crusades, turn men's attention aside very long. For under arms, millions of workers are educated in idleness, irresponsibility, and carelessness of property rights and human life; and emerging from the trenches they are more hungry, less patient, and less scrupulous than before, ready to snatch at new grievances that have grown up behind their backs. The great wars have always engendered more passions than they can possibly allay.

Nor, again, are the workers likely to be carried away by our curious modern reliance on the virtue of mere activity. More elaborate organization and increasing production are not, strangely enough, automatic guarantees of a happier and juster industrial world. The excitement of getting things done does not pay everybody for doing them. The organization employing men may be a great society for the co-operative growing and marketing of wheat, or it may be the cruelest and most selfish of private monopolies. Production may be spurred on as readily to hold a surplus of goods from the market for forcing up prices as to provide people in want with the necessities of life. Wage earners are apt to be unenthusiastic about these agencies of progress, having seen them frequently arranged to act for the benefit of the few at the expense of the many. They begin to feel that motive and use are far better tests of a thing's worth than the perfection of its mechanism.

What is going to happen to private capitalism during the twentieth century we can only guess. Will it be retired gracefully or to the rattling of tumbrils? There are a variety of possibilities. It may be that the masters of commerce and finance, abandoning competitive warfare among themselves (as they have already largely done), will erect capitalism into a closely organized militant system, far more powerful and ruthless in its rule of politics and economics than as individuals they have yet dared to be. Fascism, essentially a return to the Renaissance state, with the great men of business as its half-concealed despots, is already on this road. Elsewhere it is being watched enviously. But the result may well be a flood of reaction *a la russe,* with the end as far away as ever. It may be that the state will be gradually but surely directed at the polls to take over the whole industrial edifice, thereby merging the citizen and the worker and making political governance one with the economic. In such case the problems of genuine self-government would find themselves widely extended, for the warfare of social democracy with plutocracy would be transferred to a new and larger arena of public life. It may be that the great unions or parties of labor will in time pare away the functions of the capitalistic state (somewhat as the British Parliament has merovingianized the personal monarchy), keeping political forms for respectable figureheads, while actual power comes to be exercised by bodies chosen on a vocational rather than a geographical basis. Or it may be that through the extension of public ownership, stock distribution, steeply graduated taxes, and the whole program of social legislation, private capitalism will turn into public capitalism by the simple process of becoming universally diffused downward, through all ranks of society.

Toward each of these eventualities groups in various countries are now looking. It is likely that all of them will be realized somewhere. They are all, indeed, in process of being worked out somewhere at the present time. Economic change will no doubt find as varied, as precarious, and as exciting a career during the next hundred years as political revolution found during the last. Its details and the precise manner in which the local and general administration of industry will be developed and correlated, are beyond our sight; but if the analogies of the past and the facts of human nature are any guide, democracy will some day come in work as it has come elsewhere.

The greatest change of all will be that of the spirit. One of its aspects will be a repudiation of the venerable doctrine that competition is an assurance of freedom and the only means to progress. The competitive principle rests on the twin assumptions that men will work vigorously and intelligently for no other purpose than personal profit and that the unbridled pursuit of private gain is not incompatible with the public interest. This has been the philosophy of industrial life since the medieval "just price" and hatred of usury went out of fashion. It dominated the Industrial Revolution and in the nineteenth century received what appeared to be powerful confirmation at the hands of the evolutionists. To no other field was the biologic struggle for supremacy and survival of the strongest taken over with more eagerness than to the rivalry of economic life. The parallel is a loose one, for society as a whole has benefited largely by the striving of producers after its wealth, and competition under more or less enlightened self-interest is better than the old policy of coercion and restraint. Yet these beliefs express not a sacred law of human nature but merely an economic theory which at a certain stage of social development proved generally useful. By any other standard than the material they are untrue and vicious. For as religions and wars and crusades have given proof since the beginning of history, men will labor with far more fervor under the spur of incentives that have nothing to do with the rewards of money or what it can buy. Such passions as honor or patriotism or pity have time and again flung abroad their power to sustain men's energies and then have faded out because the masters of the hour did not know, and in their scorn were unable to learn, how to harness the vital forces of idealism to the activities of everyday life. The capitalist or labor leader is commonly contemptuous of the motives of his fellows—though he is apt to maintain that only through such motives can the general good be promoted—because he himself has done much to beat down the finer qualities of his "inferiors" and compel them to adapt their lives to his own standards. He can look ahead a few months to the advantages of increased profits or wages, but neither he nor they can comprehend the future vigor and happiness that would come from the genuine co-operation of all enlightened producers and consumers of goods. Not in anarchic self-interest but in co-operation and self-government will the final solution be found.

We speak, in all these discussions, of "labor" as a body easily defined, but the word has not always the same meaning. To the merchant, labor is apt to seem a mere commodity, subject like others to the law of supply and demand, selling itself in the dearest market and bought in the cheapest. To the engineer, labor is a machine, its value determined by quality and quantity of output and its efficiency enhanced by such intangibles as goodwill and self-expression, as well as by proper maintenance. To the statesman it may appear as a great national resource for promoting the country's interest, but needing protection and conservation as well as judicious exploitation. To the social democrat, labor comprises almost the whole body of citizens, free to express their wills in one department of life but still serfs or wards or, at most, snubbed junior partners in another lesser department, but for whom justice and humanity demand complete enfranchisement.

Labor, no doubt, is a combination of all these things, but in a wider sense it is a great deal more. For with the workers, whatever their destiny in the future, move all inarticulate, unheard, unprivileged, unorganized men in the modern world. Bound up with their fortunes are all the dumb forces rising from below, as they have risen for good or ill in every other crisis of history. And it is impossible to doubt, from our present point of vantage that somewhere in this chaos, hidden perhaps in a mountain of chaff, lies the grain of truth that will some day prevail. The philosophers may envisage it first, but only the people can bring it to fruition. In the fourteenth century social truth was not with the English barons but among the revolting serfs, in spite of the burnings and murders by which many of them terrorized the country. In the Reformation social truth was with neither the Protestant princes nor the Roman hierarchy, but scattered through the hearts of the peasants and townsmen of northern Europe, despite the practices of John of Leyden and the witch-baiters. In the eighteenth century it must have existed somewhere among the milling mobs of Paris that threw up barricades and crowded against the guillotine, but assuredly not in the king who preceded them nor the soldier of fortune who followed. So today, though any of the doctrinaire radicalisms which are the gospel of class-conscious workers may prove as false and intolerant as the Jacobin Club or the Fifth Monarchy, it must be that the elements of industrial freedom will work upward through the forces of labor, in this wider sense, rather than be laid down by benevolent masters of the capitalistic system.

Nothing has more confused the solution of economic issues than our stubborn refusal to treat them as questions of public policy. In the interests of genuine freedom the field of irresponsibility has elsewhere been gradually narrowed, so that to a large extent law and the church and government have come to be recognized as no longer legitimate spheres for the private ambition of any individual or group, regardless of their claims or apparent qualifications. The feeling has not yet become general that, in like manner, organized industry should be set beyond reach of the selfish purposes of employer or workman, man of wealth or trust or labor union, and made a field for common service as it has always become a universal function of modern life. Rights of property and contract, guarded jealously as the last strongholds of unchecked individualism, will have to be invaded and abridged and reconstructed before a just peace can be secured through the widespread extension of accountability and control among the great masses of workmen. The current methods by which these rights are attacked and defended—in most cases the only methods that lie open—are not much longer to be borne. The strike and the lockout are alike crimes against civilization; the open shop is as vicious in its partisan form as the tyranny of collective bargaining may be. This century will (we hope) show little patience with a revival of private warfare or selfish oligarchy in political life. It will have to set its face just as sternly against like motive and action in a less regulated field: the usurpation by any special economic interest of those powers rightly belonging to the people.

With the spread of this temper there will come as a matter of course—as there has already come sporadically in a few instances—the formulation of a body of industrial law, applied by courts and administered by popular officials. The Western world desperately needs a jurisprudence to cover all the varied relationships existing between men as producers and as consumers of goods, as common and statute law has long done for man as a free citizen. The machinery for its expression has yet to be created or adapted, its delicate correlation with accepted systems to be worked out, but these tasks are by no means beyond our strength. The obstructive passions and prejudices must be overborne and law ultimately be enforced by general recognition of its morality. The broader principles on which it will be based have already been conceived by men of independence and vision; the difficult labor is to win over or bring under control those interests apparently determined to resist what they consider an unwarranted interference with private affairs. We may set down as follows some of these fundamentals:

1. The rights of human beings are basic and prior to the rights of any system, organization, or commodity whatever. The men in industrial life are to be considered before the tools and the materials they work with, methods of manufacture and distribution, the financial structure over their heads. Industry is made for man, and not man for industry.

2. The primary human relation to industry is personal labor. Manual and clerical work, technical and executive skill are specialized divisions of labor. The individual possession of wealth is, in the general economic scheme, incidental, such possession being given no privileged place in society.

3. The purpose of industry is production for use—an easy phrase, but in practice subversive of the sanctity of profits, wages, interest, or any other reservation of private gain wherever these things seem to threaten the one supreme and legitimate end.

4. All workers have the same freedom and obligation in industry. They are equal not in respect of function, value to society, or monetary reward, but in opportunity to use individual talents and in responsibility for government.

5. Economic resources belong to the public. Wealth, in the shape of raw material, manufactured articles, money, credit, and goodwill, is owned by the people and administered by labor, in all its forms, as a trustee. Essential industries by nature monopolistic should be governed directly by the state; in other highly useful industries, not monopolistic, individual control and public regulation should be variously combined; the industries of luxury and amusement may be surrendered to private initiative subject only to general social legislation.

6. Industrial democracy must eventually become world-wide. Only so can currency and exchange be stabilized, regularity of production be assured, and international wars avoided.

This outline intimates how our most insistent problem may be brought under moderating and humanizing influences. The issues of economic life, just entering on the long road to civilization, have largely superseded in men's minds the issues of pure politics, already some distance along that road. Yet the freedom looming ahead of us is not to be won or maintained in a vacuum: it will become part of a social organization already old and elaborate and must be woven in with those strands already worked into the fabric. What effect it will have on law, and law on it, has been suggested. Liberty of thought and expression must be enlisted in its service and will be immensely strengthened by its victory. But most of all is the industrial settlement bound up with the future of political democracy.

There is a curious parallel, as we have pointed out, between the position we find ourselves in and that of England during the seventeenth century, when religious liberty and free government had to be reconciled and interadjusted. Somewhat as Hampden or Halifax saw that they could not separate conscience and the church from the new statecraft toward which they were working, so our leaders are finding that there is a continual and undeniable osmosis going on between political and economic issues. Political machinery, turning in an airtight compartment, is alone available to attack the economic problems crying for solution. In an earlier time such civil and religious liberties as existed proved a mockery under political despotism. We, too, are beginning to see the difficulty and the danger of professing democracy while we maintain autocratic control in industry. How the process of interaction between these two planes of life may be directed to the public interest will be the concern of the next two or three generations. Prediction would be futile, but if the work is well done industry and government will come out of the ordeal as beneficently changed as the civil and ecclesiastical polity of England were changed between the Tudors and the house of Hanover.

For whether or not political and economic life merge in outward form, they must merge in spirit before the plenary, socialized democracy of the future can be achieved. Our present universal ballot and bill of rights are not enough; our present government, with its disquieting rigidity in the face of the growing economic consciousness of all peoples, has shown itself inadequate to express their deepest interests. A vast task that calls for statesmanship of a new order is before us, the weaving together of the diverse social strands of our lives into a whole that shall be directed and preserved by the intelligent suffrage of all men.

CHAPTER VI

THE HISTORIC SETTING

The previous broad outline traces the course of that passion for freedom which our Faustian society has followed during the last five or six centuries. Its way through the modern world bears traces of a true evolution and certain elements of progress. On each new level, with different weapons and under different names, a variation of the same battle is fought over. The authority of civil law, the free play of opinion, government answerable to the common will—these are the landmarks of our civilization, to which the twentieth century may succeed in adding the principle of democracy in work. The first two were charters of the modern man, releasing him from the cramped corporate life of the Middle Ages; self-government and our rising economic unrest, turning away from the excesses of personal liberty, have spoken for the rights of men in new communal relations. The complete triumph of individualism at any epoch of history would have brought anarchy; the complete triumph of centralized power would have brought stagnation. True freedom has swung between these two extremes in its perpetual liberation of human interests and desires. As the need arises, it inclines now toward one and now toward the other, maintaining thereby a vigorous and consistent mean, yet recognizing always that society exists for the individual and not the individual for society.

Nevertheless, social liberty is not many but one. We have tried to look in turn at four different phases of its growth as each comes to dominate the world's interest in certain decades or centuries. But the separation is after all unreal, because all the great revolutions have dealt in some measure with all four aspects, and every specific reform will be found to involve two or more of them. Since the integrity of each depends on all those that have gone before, a denial of freedom in one department of life will inevitably endanger the whole structure.

The maintenance of this integrity in a changing world demands from the protagonists of liberty a continual shifting of ground. Since the radical reform of yesterday becomes the convention of today and the vested interest of tomorrow, the man who stands precisely where he stood twenty years ago, or where his grandfather once stood, may find that he is no longer a revolutionary but a pillar of society or perhaps a bourbon. Wave after wave of revolt has risen out of the darkness, won its victory, ruled, been absorbed into privilege, and then in turn been dethroned and replaced by newer, fresher forces of revolt. The center of gravity creeps upward, with the highest layer of society always in some hazard of toppling back into the mass. Every social order has begun to court destruction at the point where it has presumed its own permanence, for there is no illusion of permanence without repression; and repression, though it may drive the timid into silence, has always fired the brave or the reckless to rebellion. The ideal lives, while the institutions and the classes once embodying it fade and pass.

The great upheavals have taken a curiously parallel course. There is the oppression of the old system, long suffered in apathy and ignorance but challenged quickly enough when a certain level of enlightenment has come, whether specific abuses happen at that moment to be greater or less. There are the prophets who inspire a temper capable of meeting and worsting tyranny on its own grounds. There is the gradual gathering together of men from below, with one primary purpose and behind them a hundred different motives and methods of exploitation. There is swift culmination: the springing up of men for the hour, shedding of blood, the collapse of the system. Then a succession of new leaders, each more radical and less widely supported than his predecessor, ends with the rise of an adventurer who closes the revolution by swinging its distracted forces into a peremptory path of his own choosing. Then follows failure, the full sweep of reaction, destroying all that has immediately gone before and restoring for a time the semblance of the original order. And last comes the quieter period of fulfillment, when, sometimes almost unheeded, the real liberties that have been half-won and lost again are once more made secure for the future. The Peasants' Revolt passed through these stages, the English civil war, and, only a little less clearly, the troubled life of the Reformation in more countries than one. The French Revolution stands as the perfect type. In our own day Russia has started dramatically on the same process; it remains to be seen whether her future history will complete it.

None of the great modern campaigns for liberty has yet closed; they are all in various stages of completion. Yet the main line of emphasis traced shows a true succession of events which at times overlap. Serfdom was disappearing while the tyranny of the church grew more intolerable; toleration came when the abuses of despotism were exasperating the peoples; the Australian ballot was coincident with the labor spy and the twelve-hour day. Centuries have gone into the making of these conflicts whose crises have seemed to mark not victory but failure. The peasants' risings brought only a tightening of the bonds of villeinage, the Reformation a deluge of religious bigotry, the French Revolution a recrudescence of personal government. Today the communist regime in Russia may well be giving private capitalism a new lease of life. The extremists and the lost leaders have alike paved the way for reaction. Nowhere is the pathos in the continual defeat of man's aspirations for a better order more plainly seen than in the swamping of these movements by the doctrinaire or their diversion by the idealist turned opportunist. The blows dealt by Robespierre and Napoleon to the half-aroused humanism which, in their day, was attempting to work itself out through political channels, have been dealt in every age, by other "new men," to the more generous forces of freedom. Yet in the end a France which in some degree fulfills Mirabeau's ideal has won against Napoleon's and Robespierre's, just as the Russia that Kerensky failed to evoke may some day prevail over the inverted despotism we are witnessing at present.

These cycles furnish parallels not only in the drama of events but in its chief actors. The most vivid history is biography: certain men sum up and exemplify a whole era or class of interests. There is, for example, a true succession in such tyrants as John of Gaunt, Richelieu, Metternich, and (shall we say?) Jay Gould; in radical enthusiasts like Etienne Marcel, John of Leyden, Camille Desmoulins, and Karl Leibknecht; in unhappy monarchs like the Charles and Louis and Nicholas who were sacrificed as scapegoats for the sins of stubborn oligarchies. The relations of Robespierre and Lenin to their masters, Rousseau and Marx, bear witness to the dynamic power of two brilliant social philosophies. To such prophets as Langland and Erasmus, ironic or bitter though some of them were, one reaches back for the clearest sense of what was happening to the world in their time. They were the truest humanists, seeing through and beyond the conflict raging about them, holding with more or less steadiness the vision of what man might possibly become in face of all the disheartening things he actually was. Neither the democratic revolution nor the industrial turmoil of our own day has produced a single figure to be compared with them.

Types of mind remain constant amid the diverse and changing issues that modern men have been called upon to face. Opinions of all hues from the blandest white to the most lurid red range themselves about each new question. There is every degree of sense and nonsense, every shade of disinterestedness and innocent rationalization and casuistry. Conservatism can usually be imputed to those who have, or are striving for, privilege in high places and to those who feel that their livelihood depends on maintenance of the *status quo.* The conservative is likely to be rather toughminded, with a strong sense of order, a weak critical faculty, and a willingness to pay a high price for peace. He is commonly actuated by fear or habit—when not simply by selfishness—is loyal in a defensive way to the great principles, institutions, and men of yesterday, and content to adapt himself passively to the social milieu into which he was born. The English Tory of 1832 who did homage to the names of Ridley and Hampden while he thundered against extinction of the rotten boroughs has his heir today in the man who praises Washington or Jefferson while he looks askance at international disarmament or the rise of shop councils. Such men are apt to think of liberty as something captured once for all by their ancestors and bottled up for the quiet enjoyment of future generations.

The radical, on the other hand, is more often an idealist, imaginative and sympathetic by nature, deficient in historic sense, with an alert and elastic mind that too often hardens into the dogmatism of revolt. So long as the end can be gained he is willing to let the gaps be filled in or left open as may be. His attitude is usually traceable to some form of social maladjustment or to lack of security. Whether self-interest is a commoner or stronger motive in him than in his adversary is not easily to be determined. One is accused of greed and the other of envy, and both are often guilty, though it would

seem that the burden of refutation should lie with those enjoy-
ing the good things and the high places of this world while
they argue.

Both these social attitudes have been erected into a species
of religion. But while the religion of conservatism becomes a
fat, if stubborn, deference to the god of things as they are, the
religion of radicalism is a fierce faith responsible for many of
the great achievements and catastrophes of history. The spirit
of sacrifice, which creates and sustains popular revolutions,
can be followed through the crusades, the rise of the monastic
orders, the wars of the churches, and the wars of the nations
to its present expression in those extreme socialistic and communistic movements which have shown such startling growth
during the last seventy-five years. The discipline, the fervor,
and the insistence on doctrinal orthodoxy, once the marks of
the churchman, belong now to those secular enthusiasts who
have devoted themselves to a very different sort of salvation
for the world. It is the Puritan temper carried to its logical
end, and the more it changes the more it remains the same.
Reckless of self, it has always surrendered the individual to
the idea. There is, of course, a good deal of fanaticism, moral
pride, and downright cruelty mixed up with it. Though it
may open a way for freedom, freedom is not apt to flourish
under its rule.

The man who usually wins out in the end is the liberal—
though the end may not come until he has been shot down
by one of the extreme factions as a traitor or a trimmer. In
reality neither, he is a fair-minded person who wants and is
sometimes able to combine order with progress. Like many
of the most effective reformers, he is likely to be conservative
by temperament but radical by conviction. When these clash
he may fall into futility and be lost; but when he recognizes
that the essential quality of the old can be preserved only

through perpetual changes in form, he is able without complete upheaval to work toward greater freedom by adapting to his ideal the legalized and accepted social agencies of the time. He looks to the past a good deal oftener than those more complacent and has sometimes a disconcerting way of passing off his reforms as mere revivals of free institutions or policies that have been allowed to fall into neglect. In the midst of arms and their aftermath he is silent, or if he raises his voice he gets scant hearing; but when passion has given place to some measure of reason, he may find that fire and sword have cleared the ground for construction to begin. At best he is a mediator without being a compromiser, a champion without being a partisan, a lover of liberty without being a hater of his fellow-men.

These are the leaders; but the revolutions belong, after all, to the masses of common folk in every land who see only one step ahead and very little to either side. While their prejudices are fading and their opinions are taking shape and their loyalties are being engaged, they are eating and drinking and marrying, going about in fair weather or foul, attentive to a thousand petty conventions that will endure, however the world moves on. Most men do not live in the twentieth century at all. Their spirits cling to various favorite places along the road from the Middle Ages, though they seem to use the main highways of modern life. Their minds, clogged with old superstitions and fears, are unable to make room for reason. The great movements which fly over their heads, bringing benefits that they appropriate or ill fortune that they endure, only rarely seem to catch them up into the realm of history. Yet they are actually the atoms of which the stuff of history is composed, and though not many of them can look beyond the tiny universe bounding their immediate interests, they determine what volume and force and direction the whole may have at any particular moment. The dramatic acts which may proclaim a revolution to the world are in reality its closing phase. They set a formal seal on the unseen revolution in thought and habit that has already, if only half-consciously, been completed, in the mind of the ordinary man.

So much for the historic background of social liberty. The understanding of it ought to be of some value to us in resolving the other questions confronting our own generation. It confirms our sense of the continuity and the fundamental orderliness of life behind its apparent interruptions and confusion. It furnishes a frame of reference, as the mathematician would say, on which to hang most important events as they occur, and by which to relate them to one another and to their fixed origin. It enables us to look on our contemporary world neither as the prodigal heir of the ages nor as a new kind of swift and intricate life, but as a moving point in a history which always has been, and always will be, conditioned by the stubborn qualities of human nature. This understanding endorses the expansive dictum of Walt Whitman: "it is provided in the essense of things that from every fruition of success, no matter what, should come forth something to make a greater struggle necessary." And it shows that in the growing complexity and intensity of life there will be found wider opportunities for the seizure of power by special interests, more subtle temptations toward its abuse, more destructive forces of protest, and increasing difficulties in the formation and expression of genuine public convictions. Through all of this the drama of freedom is to be played out in the future.

Moreover, one cannot but be impressed with the slowness, the waste, and the bitterness that haunt these great grooves of change. Choosing the right one out of a thousand revolutionary ideas and erecting it into a new pillar of the social edifice has seemed to many a disheartening if not a tragic process. Are none of our future struggles to be consummated without going the way of all the others, without encountering similar triumphs of violent and intolerant forces? Must the autocrats and the libertines have their day again and again before each new victory can be assured? Or is it possible in some way to move directly toward the goal?

The answers to these questions will take us beyond the social mechanics, if they may so be called, which we have been considering. But first let us understand that the road to future liberty may be cleared by making the most of what liberties we already possess. At the beginning of this second quarter of the twentieth century the old freedom—of law, of opinion, of government—is everywhere menaced by forces of ignorance and reaction that would bring back the darker ages if they could. The promise of the newer industrial freedom is by no means clear. We shall have to fight everlastingly for these great inheritances, filling in their gaps and completing their outlines, widening the range of their influence until it becomes universal and constant in our lives. We have faith that mankind—our own fellow-men, with their eyes open and their hands unbound—can maintain the great free institutions of the past. If we have not such faith it is idle to talk of liberty at all.

CHAPTER VII

LIBERTY AND SCIENCE

We cannot think very long about the issues of the present day without striking against the ugly fact of war. War, present and future, has projected itself into the consciousness of every thoughtful man and colors all his programs and all his hopes. In a few months, as we have witnessed, it can rip away the precious and complicated fabric that has clothed the human spirit and expose it to the storms of the darkest ages. If civilization goes to smash in a more terrific conflict than the last, freedom of every sort will go too, because it will not have been strong enough to protect its own conquests.

In the famous Wellsian dictum, it is a race between catastrophe and self-control. For wars, which have almost always destroyed liberty, are chiefly the result of liberty denied or imperfectly won. Our own holocaust came out of the survival of old issues once thought safely dead and out of certain newer issues not intelligently met: the mutual jealousy and suspicion of neighbors caught in a vicious circle of defense and counter-defense; the refusal of nations and races and classes to submit themselves to any legal or moral discipline whatever; the vitiation of independent thought by all those forces of inertia and fear and privilege unwilling to abandon prejudice; the spirit of aggressive nationalism, the facts of economic ambition, ruthless competition for markets, and the menace of armaments planned originally for the commercial ambitions of diplomacy. The rubbish of barbaric lust, of feudalism, of bigotry, of autocratic power needed only a spark to set it blazing.

These anachronistic forces made the war. But except for a new and alarming power in present-day life it would never have stood out as the ominous portent it now seems. The campaigns of Napoleon, devastating though they were, bequeathed no such sinister legacy to the surviving generation. But since his day another universe has been revealed to man, physical strength of astonishing magnitude has come, and human capabilities for evil have been charged with tremendous energy. All the old vices and stupidities have found a scope undreamed of a little more than a hundred years ago. This power, giving to the illiberal agencies of the world new synthesis, and placing engines of terrific destructiveness into their hands, is to be found in the widespread use and worship of natural science as the sole measure of progress and the one way of salvation.

Here we have the second major field in which the aspirations of men have played—the understanding and conquest of the material world about them. And like conscious social reformation, science is as a great human force peculiarly a modern thing. A few men in the ancient world and two or three dim figures of the Middle Ages caught the spirit and the breadth of Aristotle's view of nature, but they made little impression on the ignorance or hostility of their time. It was Lord Bacon who, without himself meriting the name of scientist, first indicated the scope and method of modern inquiry which investigators of the following centuries have pursued with such earth-shaking results. Today it is a commonplace to say that science has remade the world. Science gave us very early in its career the compass, gunpowder, and the printing press. It has since showered on us discoveries and inventions which have become the most conspicuous and potent of human achievements. When, in the eighteenth century, science began to be applied to industry, there followed that tremendous acceleration of physical power which has continued to the present and which is hurling us headlong into a still more furious future. With our recognition of the almost illimitable power that science brings is our childlike faith in its automatic beneficence. Tragically enough, we are looking into the factories for a god (of progress) out of the machine.

True, the promise of the new knowledge was at the beginning as clear as any utopian could wish. For science is in its essence man looking at his universe, patiently assembling facts about it, formulating laws—which are merely uniformities of action—out of observed relationships, and in obedience to these laws compelling nature to do his will. The faculties of reason and imagination are its tools. And science grew up in the world of the Renaissance cleanly, with a record of accomplishment that promised to unlock doors of strength and happiness until then hardly guessed at. The ambitions of this new science were nothing less than to reveal the unknown past of the universe; to determine man's position in time and space; to make the globe as compact and conveniently arranged as a single city; to abolish drudgery; to supply mechanical contrivances for a splendid new culture; to establish a high level of uniformity over the world which would wipe out poverty and smooth away the old causes of friction and discontent. They were, in short, to bring about the complete mastery of man over his natural environment, to create a physical freedom that would scaffold whatever he built. The masters of pure science have commonly been men of high ideals and a catholic disinterestedness. Their humble co-workers, the engineers, at mahogany desks or in greasy overalls, who turn laws of nature into human power, are fitted to use their diversified talents to the highest ends of civilization. Science, one thinks, ought to have become a perfect servant of life.

A not inconsiderable part of this Herculean labor it has

performed. Through the aid of science we read history in millions of years instead of in hundreds, we lay off the universe with the speed of light for a yardstick, we talk to the antipodes in a second and go to them in a week. Our manual workers are lapped in more splendid luxury than the kings of a few centuries ago. The magic of devils and demigods has faded before the larger magic of cause and effect. The twin giants Pestilence and Famine, now toothless and crippled in their dens, creep out less often to devour the passer-by. Through science, education, public opinion, and popular government have been made possible over continental and perhaps over planetary areas. And the glowing future of science seems to us, in some moods, unbounded. Small wonder we bow down before it and its creations.

Yet it is only too painfully evident that something has been the matter. The something, it may be said at once, is human nature. Power without limit science has brought us, as Bacon promised, but not the virtue that he took for granted. It may be that science has come to adolescence a hundred or five hundred years too soon to serve humanity as it might conceivably do. For man is not yet wise enough or fine enough to make the best use of his talents. Through selfishness and lack of imagination he has betrayed science, which in turn has fatally betrayed him. Along one path it has made wasting inroads upon personality; along another it threatens to destroy the integrity and perhaps the very life of our present social order.

The second danger is the more obvious and immediate. Science has become, unescapably perhaps, the handmaid of private interest and of war. Standing as a free gift to all able to use it, it fell only to a slight extent into the hands of genuinely creative beings whose object was the welfare of all mankind. Discoveries and inventions in medicine, the one department of applied science administered by an ancient profession of high ethical standards, have formed a shining exception to the general tendency. For the most part, science has been recognized as a means less of benefiting men than of gaining control over them and wealth at their expense. The developments of modern commerce, industry, and the mechanical arts of peace have of course raised the common man's standard of life and astonishingly widened the range of his interests, but they have done so only at a staggering cost in wasted lives and money and natural resources. So far a sadly unequal battle has raged between the scattered, leaderless attempts to devote this great gift primarily to the common interest and the resolute determination of those in high places ruthlessly to exploit the power won.

Hence, both the older tyrannies whose great days are past and the younger ones which have succeeded them have found in science a pliant instrument. All the forces of privilege and oppression, the vested interests of political reaction, rabid nationalism, and predatory wealth, have grasped at its machines and employed them to further their own selfish or malignant purposes. The knowledge that might have encouraged and preserved human life has been prostituted to the more ingenious destruction of life: the finest engineering skill is impressed into the building of submarines, the chemist's laboratory becomes a factory for the compounding of poison gases and even more deadly explosives. Thus directly is war made more inevitable and more ghastly; but even the most innocent and civilizing forces are in danger of being diverted from their true uses. So long as the conscience of the world does not forbid, railroads and electric cables, coal mines and oil wells and waterfalls may serve the personal ends of a few selfish men whose opposition to the wise co-operation of all classes and peoples prevents the only free solution of our problems. As long as such men may be allowed to employ war for more ruthless prosecution of their base and personal purposes, the peace and happiness of mankind will be threatened. And still more dangerously, science's revelation to man of his amazing ascent may be perverted to a justification of brutal passions and motives that completely repudiate the Christian ethics society has so long been struggling to achieve.

The trouble is that science has made the world too small for the children racing about in it. The mechanism of our living is too complicated, too highly organized, too intricately cogged and belted to stand much more of the mischievous tampering it has had to endure. Man's reasoning powers have not kept pace with his machinery; his dim feeling for collective responsibility is beaten under and made ridiculous by the multiplicity of his agencies for wholesale slaughter. Fundamentally, it is not the improvement of tools but their use which distinguishes civilized life from barbarism. And where our tools have not been misapplied by vicious hands they have been too often dulled by stupid ones. Communication is well-nigh instantaneous and transportation unbelievably swift, yet men's minds are as far apart as they ever were—concerned with petty local affairs or obscured by hostile schemes against peoples who, though a thousand miles away, are yet too close for security. A continent has become a neighborhood, with all the opportunities for helpfulness and the quiet peace which common understanding would bring; yet the wires buzz with banalities or intrigues, and bayonets bristle at a score of sectional frontiers. Races and peoples that for many thousands of years had been differentiating themselves and withdrawing more and more completely behind their barriers of mountain and sea, have begun a swift reversal of that age-long process. By the compulsion of science, the parent of modern commerce and industry and war, they are being flung violently against one another, whether they wish it or not. Our relations are at once so delicate and so interdependent that the slightest cause of friction may set half the world on fire. It is plain truth that we are not old enough to be trusted with the dangerous toys our age entitles us to play with. A few men like Carlyle and Emerson and William Morris saw this growing disparity between our material and moral culture, but it became unhappily clear to us all during the war, when our proudest inventions turned suddenly and unimaginably frightful, as the world's finer faculties, blunted and coarsened, were dragged in the mire of savagery. This way lies madness. Sooner or later the end of everything we know as civilization will go down to destruction, should this Frankenstein, science, uninformed with a moral sense, break from our control and in sheer horror of its own fiendish aspect strike blindly to left and right.

The war brought to an end the agnostic, complacent, romantic age caught unawares. It marked the beginning of years that are fiercely skeptical, acutely miserable and weary, and stung with false catchwords, struggling still uncertainly out of their slough of despond. Yet the final accountability for this society of chaos and fear lies not with its selfish masters nor with the instruments of desolation they have let loose, but with the people who weakly suffer both. It is they who could have prevented the war—and who may prevent another great war before it is too late. But the nineteenth century worshipped the achievements of science instead of distrusting them, gathered in the streams of wealth and luxury flowing from them, and thought little of the possibilities of disaster lying in their careless acceptance of them. The lust of materialism has been our most vicious inheritance from the immediate past. A mad infatuation with speed that carried us in circles, with figures that only went on multiplying themselves, with efficiency that never stopped to ask what sort of instruments it was making effective—these marks of our boasted progress led straight to the jaws of war. So engrossed were we with things, we had little time to imagine what things could do to us.

From a good many of us they were filching our birthright as free and responsible human beings. If they did not end by slaughtering us on the battlefield they sometimes found revenge in reducing us to life-long servitude. Samuel Butler saw some time ago that machines were beginning to tyrannize over man, and he draws a prophetic picture of the time when men will become mere parasites crawling among the great engines of their creation, helpless degenerates retaining only the passion to feed, and take food from, the monsters which shall have become the center of their world. It remains to be seen how human feelings and thoughts and ideals will fare in an age that increasingly places its trust in mechanical processes. The bookkeeper on his stool, the sheet tin worker before his punch, the sailor crouched within the steel shells of a submarine, all have lost the Antaean vigor that comes from contact with the elemental things of the world; they spend their days in a tense and unreal atmosphere which a few generations ago would have been thought decidedly inhuman. Only too often personalities emerge twisted or broken, with phobias and passions or with dead fires not to be kindled again. Each step in the growth of knowledge and technique, say the psychologists, brings with it an increase of strain which develops so quickly we are unable to meet it with adequate adjustments of habit or morals. There often seems, on the surface at least, something fatal in the achievements of a science at war with the personal world we have slowly become used to living in.

But we have begun to see both the social and the individual menace and are groping for a way out. The decades ahead of us are likely to be a great battlefield for the right of science to serve life. It was the function of the nineteenth century to release a vast store of raw energy; it may well be the function of the twentieth, while increasing that energy more swiftly than ever, to control it in the common interest. The problem of peace and the problem of liberty meet in the wise harnessing of man's undisciplined mastery over nature. Just as the great social struggles of the past were concerned first with getting any sort of workable institutions and then with transforming them into institutions, so we may expect the newer struggle for material conquest to pass at length from the mere acquisition of this power to the use of it for the satisfaction of authentic human needs.

Science of itself is brute strength without morality, potent for good or ill. It is our job to use science rightly, to make ourselves truly the masters of our machines. To this end we must first be masters of ourselves. Physical freedom (and social freedom as well) will have to be sustained and directed by a human faculty concerned with the chief end of man in his earthly life, a faculty which can be called by no other name than moral freedom.

CHAPTER VIII

LIBERTY AND HUMANISM

The title of humanist, once given the world's respect, has been unfortunately allowed to fall into disuse. The name has gone because modern society does not often produce the sort of man who has a right to bear it. During more than three hundred years, from Petrarch to Milton, there lived a succession of poets, statesmen, thinkers, and men of letters whom we count among the fashioners of our present world, humanists not only because they loved the classics of ancient literature, but because they were absorbed in man, his personality and fortunes, his passions and fancies and desires, everything, in fact, that goes to make up the atmosphere of his earthly life. With Milton the great tradition breaks off. Since his death no important figure (save possibly Goethe) has sufficiently interested himself in man's whole life or devoted himself to man as man to deserve the name of humanist. The loss has been a very real one; and it is worth while to see, if we can, why this has been suffered.

The humanist, like the dinosaur and the great auk, was largely the product of his kind of world and disappeared when that world changed. It is hardly an accident that Petrarch's oldest contemporary was Dante, and Milton's younger contemporary, Sir Isaac Newton. Dante stands as the type of medieval man in the final perfection of the period's decline; with Newton we are carried for the first time into the modern world of mechanics, celestial and mundane. But between the two, between the decline of the older religious domination and the organization of the newer scientific domination, lay the period in which men found time for some unaccustomed thought of themselves. They were oppressed and frightened neither by the life to come (as their ancestors had been), nor by multiplicity of machines and the fatality of natural law (as their descendants were to be). Rather suddenly the earth had become a place worth living in for its own sake. Its inhabitants were fellow-beings with a varied personal life in the present and an exciting future ahead. For a few generations this new spirit and the positive attitude of mind which made of it something more than a luminous dream, continued to light up the lives of a considerable number of men in Europe. Its brilliance has been reflected on the world's life ever since. The Renaissance, far from being an age of Arcadian simplicity and joy, was definitely and consciously a time of transition. The old stagnant unity of Christendom had broken up, and anything might be made out of its fragments that men dared. The humanists were those intrepid souls who essayed the art of living in a free world.

Unhappily, most of them found, as most people afterwards have found, that the world was not yet free enough to make an art of living. Out of the iconoclasm of that age emerged not a cleared arena but a confusion of new conditions and new problems which have put a burden heavier than ever on human intelligence and good will. For one thing, details of civil, religious, political, and economic liberty had to be worked out—the same problems that for three or four centuries have taken up a good part of men's time. But the amazing developments of natural science have had most to do with crowding out the spirit of humanism. Our horizons have widened so illimitably, we now confront a universe in which man is only a recent comer and a precarious survivor. The sources of acknowledged power have shifted from the Creator, through man himself, to find temporary lodgment in the tremendous trinkets he constructs and in that material world out of which he has so slowly and painfully climbed. The prospect is hardly reassuring, nor is our new knowledge a very comfortable guide. Yet we have surrendered to it almost completely. Is it too terrible a thing to say that today science is winning against man? Beginning as his servant, it has come perilously near to being his master. We need not be reminded how material conditions have transformed our manner of living, nor how they affect our every impulse, our every thought, our every considered action. Whatever social liberties we may have won or may be fighting for, we are drawn deeper and deeper in the toils of our machines and the philosophies they engender in us. In spite of ourselves we are a part of all that we have met, and the powerful, crude, and often cruel implications of science are woven into the texture of our whole lives. And to what end? The philosopher says that nature, mechanically viewed, becomes indifferent to the teleological considerations of mind. The humanist would say (one hopes) that science is before very long going to pick up the civilized world and fling it to destruction in a welter of efficient barbarism.

Strong language; but it helps to state a problem crying for solution now more urgently than ever before. For if we are to be rescued from the results of our own devilish ingenuity and greediness for facts, a new sort of teacher will have to be found who will show us how to do it. I know of no name that fits, but humanist will do as well as any other, because it is a reconstructed humanism we need today—a humanism like the old in its manner of outlook on life but different in the type of cosmos and minds it confronts. In a very real sense man will have to be led back to his throne (or rather to his foot-stool) at the center of the universe. This means nothing less—and nothing more—than our rediscovery and recontrol of ourselves. To Calvin the thought of man as a priest, to Jefferson the thought of man as a citizen, were shining ideals through which society was to be made over. Held by the greatest of the seers, the thought of man, as man, in the fullness of his powers and in all the richness of his nature, was once and can be made again just as vitalizing a conception. But first we must learn to use our dangerous contrivances and our devastating hypotheses, to realize that they exist not for their own sake but for ours, that we are masters of our world in so far as we can explain it and use it to our own highest ends. However intricate, terrifying, or unmoral, things are made for us and not we for things. With this realization will come a new sense of individual and social distinction, a vital perception of our essential dignity through all the accidents invented or discovered about us. May not the figure of man, made in an image greater than he suspects, emerge from his cloud of facts as it once before emerged from his cloud of authority and magic?

This is asking a good deal. How are we to go about it? At bottom, it is a work of synthesis. Dante, we say, was the last universal poet, and Bacon the last universal scholar; since their respective days no one has professed to interpret or master our increasing stores of knowledge. But as time goes on, do we not fail more and more to digest and interrelate (two processes which perhaps amount to the same thing) those fragments of the whole which we do possess? The universe is being taken apart so minutely, its pieces are so distorted, that few of those involved in the process expect to see the pieces put together again. Science, it is true, claims to unify diversities and detect uniformities, and so it does within its various special fields; but the subdivision of knowledge proceeds farther and faster than the composition of it. Even such illuminating conceptions as evolution and radioactivity open many more questions than they resolve. It is clear that we do not get the full meaning of what we know until we can lay it beside something (no matter what it be) that somebody else (no matter who he be) knows, and say: "Here, and thus, are two common factors in the single scheme of things." We have had three hundred years and more of analysis: why may we not begin the first halting attempts to blend the parts into one consistent, rational, and ennobling whole—with man at the focal point—in which he can live in harmony and freedom? It is too big a job for anybody? We dare not admit it. For if this be so, the whole foundation of our modern life has been laid in vain.

The older humanists took off from a field of classical litera· ture because they found their aspirations and ideals better expressed in manuscripts fifteen hundred years old than in any feature of the world about them. It will have to be otherwise with us. The task demands the highest imaginative faculties ordinarily associated with art, faculties which grasp at the truth from above, rather than with the scientific mind, which prefers to induce it from below. But although the imagination is not often called into play among the humbler labors of induction, it finds full scope in the reflection which alone can integrate the data of that process. We have learned that man's spirit may be revealed in an ever-increasing diversity of ways. Science may well be one of the humanities, a door to our nature no less authentic than action and poetry and worship. Each of them has its limitations, each affords us glimpses into reality, not antagonistic but complementary. So, I think, the new feeling for man will have to make its approach through the spirit of the age: it is to be not so much a rediscovery of the old as an appropriation of the new. The temper of the modern world, born of its tutelage in the ways of observation and experiment, is impatient with any philosophy not "scientific" in form. It is useless to fight the system. Our attitude toward life is not dramatically to be dragged to light across a millennium of repression but to be wrought out of the stuff lying ready to our hands. Whether it begin consciously as science or as something else, it must put to its own uses the whole body of modern thought, just as the old thought built upon and tried to absorb the ancient culture; and its success will lie in heightening and inspiring the intellectual and moral genius of the time, translating it into a fuller language, rather than in breaking it off sharply for another. This end is best called a humanistic view of man.

The chance for success in such an attempt is greater than would have been possible a few generations ago. The last hundred and fifty years have seen an accumulation of biological and social knowledge that now claims entrance into the sacred precincts of science. It belongs to investigators standing on ground which is strictly in the older sense neither scientific nor humanistic. The anthropologist, the psychologist, the economist, the historian, and the eugenist call themselves, with some justice, scientists, because their methods of work are as exact and their conclusions as objective as it is possible to make them; but their subject matter and their aims, expressed or implied, are humane and moral. In their study they refuse to follow the old classification of "man" and "not-man." But together, they look at the whole of society, past and present, in its every variation from parent and child to the world-state. They study not only man's relationships with the natural world and with his fellows, but his dependence on those aesthetic and spiritual realities that lift him immediately to a higher sense of life. And they would directly apply their knowledge not merely to current wants, as the chemist or the engineer is likely to do, but to what they have discerned to be, in the long run, man's true needs.

Now the modern humanist is the man who can synthesize the authentic findings of the physical and biological and social sciences into a practical program toward the freedom and well-being of men over the whole world. Dr. Glenn Frank has recently and very engagingly sketched in *The Outlook for Western Civilization* an ideal portrait of such a "ringmaster of specialists." He will be any one of a hundred social philosophers who have devoted themselves to the understanding and the service of man. In the last century Comte and Herbert Spencer attempted such a task, leaving us with a new and intriguing something called sociology. One of these thinkers, of course, wandered off into a fantastic religion of humanity, and the other became unhappily entangled in the snares of cosmic evolution. Yet it is the sort of sociology we shall have to come to, if the humanistic spirit is to find effective expression. Sociology, in the larger sense of that term, is more than a bond between the old categories of man and nature. The sociologist serves, or might be conceived as serving, rather as an interpreter, harmonizer, and unifier of the two. For in the almost limitless expanse of the work opening before him, it begins to appear as the highest and widest of the sciences. In a way it stands on the shoulders of all the others, developing out of psychology as psychology develops out of biology, and biology in turn out of chemistry and physics. We are catching today the first faint glimpses of how force shapes itself into matter, matter into life, life into mind, mind into society; and so in time, if we find out what society is, we shall get over the stile and home. There is more to this business of sociology than one would think. Not satisfied to confine itself to one field, it keeps reaching out and drawing to itself those others, such as art and religion, formerly held to be on a different plane altogether. Sociology thus grows ever richer and always must go beyond the single element of knowledge it absorbs. It is aware that the whole is more than the sum of its parts; and the science of man must be as great a thing as man will ever perceive himself to be.

The whole amounts to something with which science, until very recently indeed, thought it had nothing at all to do. For because man is ineradicably a moral being at the same time and to the same extent that he is a social being, the study of human society cannot but concern itself with the active conduct of life. It has Father Damien to "explain" no less than Martin Kallikak, the Quakers no less than the Assassins; and it has an idea of what all men can become as well as of what most men are. Just so far as man at his best feels his responsibilities to the universe, so far is this new science of sociology bound to formulate the laws under which he acts and put them to work in his service. The point is that these guarded powers can, literally, make a new man of him, a man who has come to himself, who knows what he is about. This is only doing at long range what the physician does at short range when he injects an antitoxin, what the politician at still shorter range imagines he is doing when he launches a submarine to protect our coasts and slaughter our neighbors. It is only showing him how to live.

In the process the sociologist is likely to turn into what we have defined as a humanist. His new knowledge and its application involve a view of life that will break away innumerable barriers and reveal unity instead of diversity. It is no narrower prospect than this which lies in front of him. Its beginnings are already within his grasp. He has a background and a foundation. The psychologist may perhaps dispute his claim, but the two in co-operation can fill out the whole circle. One learns how man's spirit lives within him, the other shows how, with this as a basis, man may view and utilize his external world.

It is clear, therefore, that the humanistic temper, with or without the body of effective new knowledge, must lie at the heart of all of man's struggles for freedom. Looking back over the battlefield of social liberty, we can see how, in the campaigns for civil, religious, intellectual, political, and economic rights it has been the possession of those men who saw their aims most clearly, and how it pervades the great charters of our modern life. We can see likewise how the applications of natural science must come under its control if they are to be used for man's lasting good instead of for his early destruction. But there are many other fields, wide and narrow, in which his right to live a free life is being perpetually challenged by forces of ignorance or habit or superstition or private interest. The spirit of humanism may be turned on all of these by attacking their issues quietly, even informally, yet with resolution and success. These issues it attempts to surround with its own influence, applying the pressure of reason, example, social opinion, or sheer goodwill, resorting at times to law, using as much science as it knows and is permitted to use, and subjecting every institution or custom or passion it touches to the searching test of humanity.

The barriers to freedom are innumerable; but let us speak here, in a word, of a few that stand out today with peculiar sharpness. They may be called bondage to convention, ugliness, cruelty, and thoughtlessness, family disorganization, race hatred, the menace of numbers, and ignorance. Against these the humanistic spirit speaks for the worth and dignity of man's life, for the largest self-expression and fulfillment of his aspirations, for common kindliness and helpfulness and pride in action. And in so speaking, it demands a courageous facing of fact, the progressive control of fact by science, and the control of science by the sort of moral imagination that can project itself into the future.

Social convention is, of course, one of man's saving graces, but it degenerates sometimes into a vice. It would appear to be a vice when considerable numbers of men cannot freely follow their own tastes and chosen pursuits or frame their private lives wholly to suit themselves with the single proviso that no one else shall suffer for their acts. Conformity may express itself merely in the minute amenities of everyday intercourse, or it may be the dead hand of the past laid upon honesty or spontaneity or joy in the most intense and absorbing things of life. We have traveled far from the time when every man's occupation was prescribed from birth and two of every woman's four limbs were both invisible and unmentionable, but there are just as many tragic or absurd usages left, and new ones are being encouraged all the time by people too lazy to think things through or too suspicious of their fellow-men. We need today (perhaps now more than ever) a healthy defiance of the standardized thinking and feeling and conduct which this age is doing its best to impose on us. We need a series of good knock-down and drag-out bouts between Mrs. Grundy and a few contemporary Thoreaus and Lord Timothy Dexters. And these should be followed by a wide tolerance of harmless or noble eccentricity. True, we shall no doubt suffer a dozen egregious asses for every man who has some genuine originality to contribute to the common stock, but the gayety of nations will be enhanced in a world grown somber with the hue of a machine civilization. The mortality of heretics and cranks is heavier than it should be, for while we are steam-rollering the large majority who merit nothing better, there are bound to be a few irremediable casualties among the true prophets. Genius is not to be measured by unpopularity, but sometimes unpopularity may be measured by genius.

One gain from taking the conventions less seriously will be a flowering of art. Let the creative impulse now lying obscurely in the human microcosm once finds itself unhampered, the ugliness and emptiness that clutter our days will soon be transformed or swept away. Great art, says Professor White-head, is the arrangement of the environment so as to provide for the soul vivid but transient values. The aesthetic appreciation flowing from great art cannot therefore but increase the depth of personality. The arts of the past have been only too often avenues of escape from the grossness and stupidity of the actual world, esoteric means of withdrawing to a region where the multitude could not follow. They were essentially aristocratic, and they were divorced from reality. But when we learn that life in its every detail and activity is itself potentially an art and can be lived with that harmony and delight and strangeness which are the qualities of beauty, the sensitive and fearless urge to expression may well become a common human faculty. What may be termed the com-memorative arts—painting, sculpture, architecture, music, literature—by which feeling and imagination are recollected and preserved for the future, will perhaps be always nurtured by the peculiar talents of a few, though all of us may draw strength from them; but the arts of immediate and fleeting expression, of dress, of work, of play, of worship, of comrade-ship, belong to the people and are theirs to develop with what diversity and spontaneity they will. Is it too much to look forward to a communism of creative effort which will result in a general outpouring of beautiful objects and activities and lives?

Against the ancient sins of cruelty and carelessness men have always waged private war, but only in the eighteenth century did they wake to the need for collective effort against certain glaring abuses. One shudders to think of the appalling amount of misery suffered in silence and observed with in-difference in a more callous age. There is, in all conscience, plenty of it left, as one may see around the first unaccustomed corner; the bustling charity of these days has touched only

the most conspicuous festers of pain and wretchedness. Rousseau is perhaps to be accounted the spiritual father of our
humanitarianism, but it found its first effective champions in
John Howard, who woke the conscience of England to the
revolting prison conditions of his time, and in Becoaria, who
fought against heavy odds for more humane methods of
punishment. From these men to such an outstanding contemporary figure as Jane Addams lies a succession of prophets
and reformers who have devoted themselves to the development of mercy and pity toward the unfortunate as a social
policy. The forms it takes are legion: care for the sick and
needy of every sort, the great movements against slavery and
drunkenness, public health and improved living conditions,
the welfare of children, kindness to animals, recreation, popular education, a large part of missionary effort, the profession
of social work—all the diverse agencies and programs about
us. Of recent years great foundations have been created, giving
promise of becoming among the most powerful of human
institutions. The failings of the humanitarian spirit—super-
ficiality, the demoralization of those it seeks to help, its use
merely to keep unpleasantness out of sight or to prevent
inconvenient scrutiny into the sources of wealth—all are to be
overcome by turning more and more from relief to prevention, by basing action on exact knowledge instead of on undisciplined emotion, and by looking to the ultimate causes rather
than to the occasions of social ills. Above all, such a program
should recognize that it is not a substitute for social justice,
but its forerunner and its vigilant critic.

   In its wide ranging over the hills and valleys of contemporary life, humanism is brought up short against the perplexing
issues of marriage and the family. The family, through all
its transformations since primitive times, has remained basic
among institutions. Its essential civilizing task has been the

exaltation of love from a mere animal impulse to a plane on which, in the wider social world, it is able to move as the loftiest and sometimes the most powerful of man's capacities. From the broadest viewpoint the family should therefore be regarded as a great school of emotional and imaginative life, the forger, conserver, and giver-out of love, the bridge by which man has been able to span the gulf between the brutal and the finely human. Yet despite its immense cultural value it has only too often in the past been the refuge of personal despotism, cruelty to the helpless, or blindness to wider social needs, and has cramped self-expression in a thousand petty ways. Just now, owing to the sudden economic independence of women, strange urban ways of living, the surrender to large-scale industry of many ancient home activities, and the new-old revolt of youth, the family seems to be in one of its periodic states of violent flux. But whatever changes in form or function the next few generations may bring, we need fear only those in which love, conceived as the noblest of all relationships between the home and the community, shall be degraded from its hard-won position as the accepted genius of family life. Greater freedom is, of course, the avowed goal of all the new contractual and emotional relations proposed today; but humanism judges freedom less by the personal advantage or selfish indulgence it offers than by its full and final effects on all those touched by it. Not only the husband and wife, but the child and society as well, have rights in the family that must be regarded as indefeasible. No one party may be served at the expense of any other. The perennial question in the domestic sphere is finding a mean between unbridled authority and anarchy. How the best of the new liberty and the old responsibility can be conjoined in a stable yet inspiriting relationship is a problem worthy the best efforts of the twentieth century.

Racial enmity, ugly glimpses of which have been given during the past few decades, is a new thing in the world. Hatred of the casual stranger, the slave, or the invader is as old as history, but not until recently have whole peoples, of the most diverse origins and cultures, confronted one another inescapably as neighbors, rivals, and potential enemies in the struggle for a place in the sun. It has been said that the conflict between social classes lies in the primary economic sphere; the conflict between nations is economic and political; while the conflict between races is at once economic and political and deeply human, reaching down to the very roots of our nature and feeding on stubborn and unreasoning prejudice. This is one of the most ominous of all clouds on our horizon; certainly no world-wide, or even continent-wide, program of human betterment can be carried through that does not reckon with the grim fact of race hatred. There is no easy laying of the specter: it did not rise with the pseudo-scientific dogma of Caucasian or Nordic superiority, and it will not fade should that dogma be forgotten and all races shown to be inherently equal in cultural capacity. Yet the fact that children as well as some large human groups are immune to this antagonism, shows that it is not universal but depends rather on vicious teaching and certain conditions under which various peoples come into contact. It has been born, in part, of suspicion and ignorance and envy, diseases which can be considerably weakened by subjecting them to the same social antitoxins that we are learning to apply to the causes of enmity between hostile nations and classes. The deeper layers of instinct and emotion, deriving from we know not what primitive source, can be touched by no formal remedy, however finely carried out. Whether the social distance between races will ever be annihilated is not now clear. It can only be by a conscious act of will on the part of each

individual now guilty of perpetuating it. It is likely to be one
of the last vices to fall before that temper of human brother-
hood—itself a combination of knowledge and self-control
guided by high ethical principle—which can recognize no
such denial of personality.

Before racial peace can be realized we shall have to face
resolutely the problem of population. To this one problem, indeed, most of our others in the end reduce themselves. The
rapid doubling of the world's population during the nineteenth century has created or greatly intensified a good many
of the issues we are struggling with today. Our intolerance,
our distrust of practical democracy, our industrial warfare, our
hatreds and jealousies of other peoples, our panicky wars are
all due largely to the fact that we have suddenly begun to
feel crowded on a shrinking planet. And if we are at length
to be overwhelmed by sheer weight of numbers, millions of
human beings crowding on too fast to be made into decent
members of society or even to be fed, all the past achievements of liberty will avail us nothing. It is a race between
culture and population, a duel of intelligence with the rising
tide of barbarism. Out of the confused discussion of the present there seem to have emerged only three ways of preserving
both our civilization and our humanity. We shall probably
end by adopting all three: limiting population by voluntary
means, improving its quality through deliberate breeding, and
turning to simpler ways of living. Only in that way can we
prevent too severe a strain on the material and cultural fabric
of modern life and produce men capable of meeting the demands made upon them. Realization of these first two policies,
with all the practical measures they involve, is a delicate business, in the course of which we must not allow present justification of injustice, cruelty, or violations of the finest moral
sense on conjectured grounds of future good. The third, that

of actually drawing in our belts so that we and our children may keep the essentials of freedom within a narrowed income, will prove a severe trial for a society such as ours, founded on the ideal of "prosperity." But, barring some incalculable access to chemical or mechanical energy that will deliver us forever from all concern for the morrow, retrenchment will have to come. We cannot continue indefinitely to squander our capital as we have been doing. With our higher thinking must come plainer living, which we shall need not a little fortitude to accept.

But as a prelude to all these victories, ignorance and superstition will have to go. With clearer knowledge of the laws by which man lives must come their incorporation into the common heritage. Education is, therefore, humanism in process of perpetuating itself. Man is not automatically true to his own better nature, but he can become so as a result of training and discipline. The still unfinished campaign of the last century and a half for enlightened, universal, and intellectually free schooling is one of the brightest chapters in the modern warfare of the spirit. The first work of education is to pass on to another generation the best that has been thought and felt in the world and, somehow, to see it embodied in new lives; education's still higher office is to evoke the creative intelligence that shall be able to mold society to a finer form. Hence it can never be erected into a closed system or expressed once for all in a formula; it must be fluid and experimental. If we are committed to the idea of progress we cannot get on without leadership; and we cannot have wise leadership without periodic revolutions in our ways of thinking. The youths we teach today will set new ideals of thought and action on which the education of tomorrow will build until the men it produces form still other ideals for the education of the day after tomorrow. But though experimental in means, its aim remains constant—to narrow the frontiers of ignorance by attacking them boldly. It must look for thoroughgoing conquest and control of man by himself. Only so shall we gain that most precious of human possessions, universal self-respect.

Beyond doubt, the free society of the future is to be founded on the dignity and vigor of its great inheritances. Law and opinion, government and industry and science can be made the vehicles of a better way of life; but these things are after all nothing more than social mechanics whose value is to be measured through the collective purpose of those in any age able to use them. It is to the spirit of humanism, illuminating and informing all these agencies, that we must look for guidance. The world of tomorrow will be essentially what its men are; the social order to come will sink its deepest roots in the heart. The achievement of this fuller liberty will come through the education of men in the knowledge of themselves, and through their power of acting on that knowledge to affirm the capacity for good in human nature and the responsibility of society as a whole for its own welfare. Thus we will secure the release of those deepest hidden faculties which we have unknowingly possessed, the emergence, from behind all the abnormalities and preoccupations with which his long road has been cluttered, of the man genuinely worthy of freedom. As freedom has been declared and nurtured for so many other ends, so now it may be declared and nurtured in the service of man as splendid man. Hope rests in his willingness to make himself normally and steadily what, by shining intimation or the faithful interpretation of fact, he knows himself genuinely to be. So the progress commonly conceived in terms of social contract and material invention may become the framework of a renaissance that will sweep us far beyond the customary limits fixed for human percep-

tion, human power, and the possibilities of human brother-
hood. Since our possessions have been too often our limitations, we may well imagine a society in outward respects more
simple, less hampered by its restless needs for money and
things, and happier in the unfolding of those generous impulses which most truly reveal its heart.

CHAPTER IX

LIBERTY AND RELIGION

The supreme expression of liberty is to be found in religion. The last and largest act in the mutual adjustment of man and the cosmos is carried through in the realm of the spiritual and the superhuman. He has found freedom through contracts and institutions which subserve his needs, in tools which he learns to use for his own good, in the self-knowledge and self-control of the humanistic temper; he finds it finally in that harmony of his deeper nature with the whole universe which can best release him from the bondage of fear and put the fruits of the spirit in its place. He projects the values of human personality into the world at large; and he draws from the central Personality, moving through every atom, assurances that are the insignia of spiritual freedom. Out of this high intercourse between God and man come momentous, if but partial, answers to his ancient questioning and an abiding sense of love and joy and peace that satisfies the craving of his heart.

Religion, so conceived, is the chief end of man, the noblest and, in its perfection, the most remote of his goals. It is at once an individual and a social concern. As an inner experience through which each of us may find new life in the apprehension and the love of God, it must always remain an adventure of the solitary heart of man in search of an ever-lasting home. The deepest values of life are qualitative rather than quantitative; they can be expressed only in terms of personality, and are arrived at neither through knowledge nor through business, but through the silent, direct activity of the spirit. The great masters of the religious life have all withdrawn themselves for a time to the desert, physical or psychic, in their quest for ultimate reality.

Yet they went into the desert from the world of men, and they came out to become a part of that world once more. Religion cannot remain long divorced from humanity. Personality itself, the raw material with which it works, is in part a social product, assembled and selected from all that man has thought and felt and done in his age-long ascent. In the matrix of society are formed the men who some day strangely discover that they possess a spiritual nature. This is not to say that religion has been evolved by society or depends for existence on it: religion is from the beginning an essential and inexpungeable part of man's being; but the tissue of conventions and aspirations amid which every one of us finds his place affects deeply the kind and quality of his religious experience. Personality, however, becomes in the end something very different from raw material. Heightened and transformed, it is the thing which religion exists to create, the central fact of the universe, the be-all and the end-all of existence. It becomes the fullest manifestation of life that we are capable of conceiving. And so religion gets back to earth. Its applications must of necessity be social and humane. As Jesus said, the only effective way to love God is to love man: we serve Him by serving the least and the greatest of His creatures. And in doing this we build up for them and for ourselves a new world of transcendent and enduring values.

Hence it should be clear what relation religion bears to humanism, and so to science and social reformation. It alone can furnish the inspiration, the motive power, the spiritual sanction for that devotion and reverence for men out of which is born a better common way of life. A humanism acting for man as a superior beast, having no dealings but with his fellows and with the visible world of nature, is futile and impotent: it must act rather for man as part of an intelligible and purposeful universe, toward the completeness of which he contributes by working out, as a divine being, his high and obscure destiny. That is to say, it must act for man as a child and sometimes as a comrade of God. There can be little strength of virtue in a religion of humanity which, in attempting to compound the life of man as it has been lived in all places and all times into an object of veneration, appropriates the product of authentic religion without acknowledging the debt. No: mankind is comprehended and fulfilled only by getting outside itself, by reference to the superhuman powers that envelop the spiritual existence of all its members. Not the worship of our own unhappy, perverse, and divided fellow-men, but the infusion of a very different sort of religion into their individual and thence into their common life will be the means of guiding the race on a broader and deeper course through the future.

Humanism is therefore the other half of religion, its practical application in society. The knowledge and the love of God finds its natural and necessary completion in the knowledge and the love of men: religion must use humanism for its expression. And, *per contra,* through humanism a new and inspiring view of what religion truly is may be attained; our insight into man can fortify and interpret our vision of God. We are led down from the divine to the human; and we are also led up from the human to the divine. Our immediate perception of reality furnishes us a standard and type to apply to relations with our fellows, and we carry back the loftiest of earthly passions and achievements and ideals to make vivid our picture of the unseen world. These two processes have been interacting and sustaining each other since the beginning of history. To some of us the first, to others the second process, will appear the more vital and inevitable. The genuinely religious man will see in them an example of the subtle osmosis going on throughout nature and the universe.

And with humanism go hand in hand all the other instru-
mentalities of liberty we have been discussing. As humanism
uses science and social reformation for its own ends and in
turn is strengthened by them, so must religion, through the
humanistic temper, use and find inspiration in these great
agencies of freedom, gathering to itself the whole range of
human knowledge and activity. As for science, it holds a
high and splendid place among the instruments of religion,
but it remains an instrument and can never become a source
of independent authority. Its facts are but facets of religious
truth, its broadest generalizations but a mode of religious
thinking. Science is limited in two directions: it cannot know
first causes or final events, and it cannot get to the bottom
of personality, so that the values it creates have not the universal and absolute character of religious values. Instead of
pitting the two against each other as enemies or trying in an
easy way to "reconcile" them, we shall have to begin finding
out what their real relationship is. When the astronomer
Kepler had for the first time worked out the true motions of
the planets, he is said to have exclaimed: "Now I am thinking
the thoughts of God after Him!" Today Dean Inge speaks
for a considerable company of intelligent men when he says:
"I believe that in science has come the chief revelation of the
will and purposes of God that has been made to our generation." The laws of the physical sciences we accept without
question, not only as consistent with the divine governance
of the universe, but as an amazing discovery of its power and
grandeur. Just now we are feeling our way through the findings of biology (to some a stumbling-block in the way of
religion), which to many have begun to make a still more
magnificent disclosure of God's methods. The nascent sciences
of man have still to find their place in the scheme of a
spiritual world; yet it is certain that in the end they will find

it, despite the rivalry or contradiction they may be assumed to create. We are no longer concerned that the four corners of the earth should be ensphered or that the rocks should be laid down everlastingly, but some of us are still considerably worried about the gill-slits in the human embryo. Few have gone so far as to wonder what the psychology and sociology of the future may do to our comfortable ancestral views of man's mental and social life and the precise manner in which they glorify God. Yet religion, purifying science and being purified by it, must learn, as humanism is learning, to encompass the whole body of modern thought and subdue it to its own purposes, as it once before encompassed and subdued and was purified by the philosophy of the Greeks. "All knowledge," said Coleridge finely, "begins and ends in wonder; but the first wonder is the child of ignorance, while the second wonder is the parent of adoration."

So with the great struggles for social liberty. They, too, are, sometimes in spite of themselves, a part of the same unity. Religion, we say, speaks directly to the heart. The social gospel is only a by-product of the individual gospel, but it is an essential by-product. The truly religious man may not be indifferent to the institutions that determine the character of society; and no society can remain whole or free that cuts itself off from the loftiest source of health and freedom. This is by no means the platitude one might suppose. It has been a tragic fallacy of many churchmen and many reformers to assume that religion and social progress have nothing to do with each other. The sincere and high-minded reformers would have us believe that spiritual things are on a wholly different plane from the material, but in divorcing the affairs of Cæsar so completely from the affairs of God they give to any potential Cæsar the rulership in this world and place religion in a position of silent acquiescence in despotism and misery. It is, of course, true that the mystic and the personal evangelist may know God in a peculiarly direct way. Yet their lives are not fully rounded unless they can enter as well into the larger life of man in society. Only the most absent-minded or the most superbly confident individual can find it possible to dream of love or live unquestioningly in a world of haters—a world that sees feudalism or a vicious political and economic order crushing the life of his fellow-men. Among a few saints and heroes the spirit is able to pour contempt on the needs of the flesh, but the great mass of men require a certain measure of self-respect and material well-being before they can sustain the religious life. This is not to deny that suffering and sacrifice may often lead more surely to the gates of truth than a stalled ox and a full dinner pail. But there will always be plenty of suffering and chances for sacrifice without looking for them in human oppression.

Certain radicals, on the other hand, in their war on the superstition and hypocrisy that accompany social abuses, have tried to get rid of religion altogether and turn progress into the frankest sort of materialism. This, too, is a groping in the fog of half-truth. They are, no doubt, more honest than those who drift to the same end under cover of respectability. In all conscience, let us have done with the shame of ecclesiastical or theological systems that put form before truth; but religion simply will not be separated from life. This social faith, narrow and fierce as it may be, is a species of religion, one of those spurious religions, to be sure, which inevitably slip in to take the place of the genuine, when the true religion has been driven out. The fatal error of this theory is its attempt to deny the highest and most indestructible part of human nature.

Moving, as it does, along a narrow path toward certain limited ideals of physical and social satisfaction, it leaves no room for that less tangible, unbounded idealism out of which man's fullest life has always emerged and which can never be wholly atrophied. The freedom of human institutions and systems, of whatever sort, must minister to man's spiritual freedom and in turn serve as the outlet for energies generated by it. Whatever degree of liberty he achieves upon earth is at once the sustenance and fruit of his liberty in another realm. As with science, religion must purify and be purified by the forms in which he casts his common life.

And the end of it all? "Love, and do as you like," said St. Augustine. Can we refuse to see the last measure of social truth in the deeper unity of all mankind? Is such unity to come otherwise than by the power of love? There lies the ultimate dynamic of liberty, beyond which no *ubermensch* will ever go. Where and how it is most surely to be found we may learn from the philosophers, the poets, and the prophets, the slayers of illusion and the champions of reality, from all the makers of magic words which hold some little fragment of their magic those who come after. It is found in the breath of that Spirit of which ours is the clouded image, in the touch of the Reality outside ourselves, through one of the countless shapes in which it is made manifest. Contact may be won through the world of nature, which is God's handi-work—alike the star-clouds of Andromeda and the plunging surf and the weed by the roadside—whether one views the scene about him with the kindly glance of Wordsworth or the seared, triumphant eyes of Job. It may be won through the world of man, who is what you please, a forked radish, a brute perverted to self-consciousness, an immortal fallen into sin, yet a creature who carries in his breast an inextinguishable spark of the divine fire. He may go lower than the beasts, but he also goes higher than himself: there is in music the muted voice of God, in painting are His veiled features, in poetry His shrouded finger may be writing truth on our clay-shuttered walls. More than that, there is somewhere in the personality of every man, if we search and select and interpret with sufficient insight, His very presence; and in one who is the type and pattern for all the race, His presence without the need of searching or of selection or of interpretation. And finally, communion comes most perfectly through the immediate intercourse of spirit with Spirit, in which the barriers of sense are breached and for certain rare moments of time victoriously passed. Nature, man, my own heart: these are the three great roads to reality, to the inmost shrine of love.

The implications of this for the individual cannot here be traced. Our concern has been with his wider life in society. And for society the end of the long progress of liberty is not easily to be discerned. This great adventure, begun in the darkest ages of the past, is perhaps always to remain a process, a becoming, in which new vistas stand revealed as the old ones close behind. It may be enough to know that the journey is always under way, that somewhere there are always those who have given their lives to the achievement of one more step along the path of freedom. Responsibility is theirs and ours. The character of society is made by us and not for us: we must work out our own common salvation with knowledge and reverence. Today it is more difficult than ever before to withstand the forces of diversion and dissipation, harder to look steadily at man himself through all the vestitures of occasion and circumstance wrapping his spirit and clogging its vital energies. Yet unconquerably he is the master of his fate, the captain of his soul. There are no claims superior to the demands of his own highest nature.

So we come back to the better world of men's dreams and labors. It is a great dream to envisage the new order—one in which the cruel, weak, and fearful powers no longer enslave life, but in which the great forces have been turned toward

release of the spirit. This is an apocalypse worthy to set beside
that of the old man alone with his vaulting imagination on
Patmos while the machinery of universal empire reverberated
about him and was imperceptibly sloping to its fall. In the
last analysis the conflict for human freedom fuses into the
immemorial problem of good and evil; only when the one
has been forever solved will the other be brought to a close.
A truly free society cannot by its very nature bear with any
of the repressions and injustices and stupidities creating the
unrighteousness of our present life. Such a society is surely
not altogether beyond our sight; a freer world than that which
any previous generations have been born into is ours for the
effort of attempting it. Men will have to be leavened to catch
some glimpse, blurred or fragmentary though it be, of the
great ideals of liberty, to think clearly about them, to have
faith that they are progressively possible of realization, to give
years to the task of making them come true. The vision is
futile and bitter enough of itself. Men will have to take it
into the mines and sweatshops and committee-rooms, the
grain fields and the battle lines—every spot where, by the
sweat and thought of men and women, the social fabric of
our day is being woven, and there put in the hearts of their
brothers some understanding of the freedom, the harmony,
and the unselfish devotion which are the foundations of a
finer way of life. The better world, the millennium, the Kingdom of Heaven, if you will, is not an era of the future; it is
here and now for those who have learned how to bring it
into being for themselves, and it is momently being created in
the lives of others throughout the world. "Turn but a stone
and start a wing": our spirits are, if only we knew it, so-
journers in no strange land. That this land is the natural and
rightful inheritance of all humankind will be perhaps the
most worthwhile discovery of our children.